COUNSELLING PSYCHOLOGY MEETS MULTICULTURALISM IN THE TWENTY-FIRST CENTURY

{. . . Inside AMeriCa . . .}

COUNSELLING PSYCHOLOGY MEETS MULTICULTURALISM IN THE TWENTY-FIRST CENTURY

FIRST WRITTEN AS AN INDEPENDENT RESEARCH PROJECT

By Theodus J. Jordan

Submitted to
Dr. Edward McGrath, Professor
Faculty Advisor, Counseling Psychology Department,
CAMBRIDGE COLLEGE

In Partial Fulfillment for the Degree of

MASTERS OF EDUCATION
COUNSELING PSYCHOLOGY

CAMBRIDGE COLLEGE
CAMBRIDGE, MASSACHUSETTS
DECEMBER 2005

COUNSELLING PSYCHOLOGY
MEETS MULTICULTURALISM IN THE TWENTY-FIRST CENTURY

iUniverse books may be ordered through booksellers or by contacting:

iUniverse
1663 Liberty Drive
Bloomington, IN 47403
www.iuniverse.com
1-800-Authors (1-800-288-4677)

ISBN: 978-1-4917-8378-8 (sc)
ISBN: 978-1-4917-8379-5 (e)

Print information available on the last page.

iUniverse rev. date: 01/03/2017

PROLOGUE

[Question 1] **Did you know,** that in America, the phenomenon and discourse of **"Counseling Psychology"** as a discipline has been presented largely from the prism of a 'mono-cultural' perspective since Sigmund Freud-19th Century (pg 13)? As you know Freud is known as the Father of modern-day "Psychoanalyses". This author does not attempt or desire to give the impression of challenging the works of Sigmund Freud in any way, but Freud is mentioned here only to show the relevance of his work to the origin of the term **"Counseling Psychology"** (pg.31). This term has been chosen to present the title of this author's most recent book (work): *"COUNSELING PSYCHOLOGY", MEETS MULTICULTURALISM IN THE TWENTY-FIRST CENTURY!!!!*

[Question 2] **Did you know that as such, "Counseling Psychology" being presented only through a 'mono-cultural' perspective since Freud,** has not been as effective as it could in reaching people of diverse backgrounds (pg.25)? Why not? Because the relationship between the subject and the analyst, the doctor and the patient, the practitioner and client, the therapist and the patient, the counselor and the examined, the teacher and student, the minister and member (parishes), the officer and soldier, the prisoner and guard, has changed. **diversity** has been identified as essential to the understanding of **human nature . . . .** **the** understanding of **"diversity"** is essential to the ultimate **"healing"** of the individual.

Diversity must now be reconfigured into the **"healing equation".** Therefore, **"Counseling in Psychology",** now needs to be **reset** from its **"mono-cultural" perspective** in order to understand its 21st. Century client. Hence, a more in-depth inquiry into the *multiculturalistic* perspective, experience, value-system, nature, and background of the client is imperative (pg.44). In his book—*"Counseling Psychology", Meets Multiculturalism In The Twenty-First Century,* the author--Theodus J. Jordan--points out how **"Counseling Psychology"** when approached from a **'multi-cultural' perspective** instead of a **'mono-cultural' perspective** in today's America, could reach more people of diverse background with more effective results (pg.44).

[Benefits]

A *multicultural* approach to "Counseling Psychology" is paramount to the achievement of a **"more cohesive and perfect union"** within our still developing **"democracy"**. The prospective counselor/patient/ client-relationship can produce a more measured experience while achieving a more significant and positive results—more often, with less difficulty, because the advice given is **internalized** more completely when **diversity/ Multicultural** perspectives, are recognized and valued (pg.47).

The author's book presents a clearer more relative approach to understanding the healing-powers within **"Counseling Psychology"** . . . **when "Counseling Psychology"** is approach from the **multiculturalistic *verve*** within **doctor/patient/client/practitioner-relationships**. For example, given the devastations of history with its ***traumatic*** impact of <u>Slavery's</u> destructive forces and denigration, dehumanization . . . and, its castigation of the human will, its annihilation of the human mind, its piercing of the heart, and breaking of spirit and conscience—these <u>forces of slavery</u> have been so absolute, and so complete in their destruction. Such meticulous sustaining designed programming ingrained into the human experience and made synonymous with the stigmatization of "skin-color" for centuries, not only erects and imprisons the individual externally through environmental forces, but crushes and sears the *psyche* with traumatic mental consequences: such as blocking and participating freely: economically, politically, educationally, equally in the opportunities that black-people have created, but earned through their laborious unpaid hands.

Such stigmatization prevents automatic and equal access, equal revenue-sharing, while forever promoting inequality, perpetuating unequal-treatment of all people-of-color. How? The indelible scaring of the *psyche*, **left from slavery's edict,** is so deeply imbedded in the soul of **Black people (or, any people**: Native American, Japanese American, Chinese American, Jewish American, Immigrant American—and other Americans) from generations to generation, cannot be de-programmed, healed on its own, by suddenly turning itself right-side-up! Without a directed one-on-one, group-by-group, face-to-face, systemic and sustained **counseling-therapeutic model**—between practitioners/clients/physician/ patient/therapist/subjects, in de-programming instructions, the process of **healing** in race-relations, "**perfecting our union**" (i.e. achieving full-Democracy) will never be achieved (pg.50).

Approaching "**Counseling Psychology**" multifariously—by valuing all aspects of the *multicultural-historical experience*—brings all groups into a "**common recognition**" of the others value system, others rights to being, others belief systems, others pains, others history-- thus, their humanity—**empathetically.** This **commonality,** as this author believes, brings about both "**equality**" and "**respect**" for all humanity (pg71). This author also believes that a **shared sense of commonality** foments a shared **sense of humanity** resulting in an investment of shared **values . . . .** Thusly, living in such a **shared common existence** produces fewer wars—**cold** or **engaged**—which brings about a **natural healing** between all races, colors, classes, genders, languages, backgrounds, cultures, and ethnicities alike (pgs.50, 51, 56).

In summary, this author's intent is to give "**Counseling Psychology**" a "make-over", or, a reversal of roles, by allowing "**Counseling Psychology**" to become **the Patient** and "**Multiculturalism**" to become the **Physician.** The therapist, the practitioner, the teacher, now has the chance to evaluate each others' role more **empathetically** than before . . . resulting in a more reliable, valued, lasting, but efficient understanding of **healing** as these two seem to accelerate toward completion in their interpersonal dance.

CONTENTS

FOREWORD

By Dr. Edward J. McGrath

I F ONE HAS had the pleasure to witness the preaching of Reverend
Theodus Jordan the reader can clearly feel the energy that is evident
in this book. Reverend Jordan examines how the counseling profession has
evolved in its understanding of society and the development of personality.
The author explores interdisciplinary views as they relate to the
interactions of individuals in professional counseling relationships and their
application in modern society.

Reverend Jordan differentiates between two terms that are commonly
used interchangeably: counseling and psychotherapy. The distinction is
extremely insightful and provocative. Each term has a specific meaning,
especially when applied in the relationship with a patient or client. Intriguing
is the section that discusses the dynamic that exists when two strangers
meet for the initial session. Throughout the chapter the author cites varied
therapeutic approaches and the paradoxes that are evident when compared
to particular times in history. The entire first chapter is a capsulated view of
the evolution of the world view of psychology and the inter-relationships of
theorists. These thinkers have been shaped by social psychological patterns.

Chapter Two is where Reverend Jordan clearly shines. His discussion on
multiculturalism begins with a discussion of what constitutes culture. The
author cites several anthropological scholars who struggle over the definition
of the terms. The reader can sense the frustration and ambiguity that
Reverend Jordan must have felt when facing a non-definitive definition of
how culture is precisely defined. With an acknowledgement of the vagaries
of definition and a conclusion that culture is complex, Reverend Jordan
explores the concept of multiculturalism.

Again, the reader can sense the ardor and passion that Reverend Theodus
Jordan possesses when attempting to formulate a distinct understanding of
the phenomena of multiculturalism and its interplay with modern living and

experience. The conflicts involved between theoretical and actual practice are examined and discussed. Of particular interest is the section that addresses the confusion in mainstream language, textbooks and academic curricula. The author cites the overgeneralizations and stereotypes are contributing forces in lowering self-esteem in particular groups of people. The chapter concludes with a powerful discussion of the paradoxes that exist in modern multicultural practice. Contradictions abound in cultural belief systems.

Existentialism, and its relevance to psychotherapy, is examined through a two-prong approach. A philosophical approach and a psycho-therapeutic outlook are discussed. Reverend Jordan cites a number of theorists through a historical and a conventional view. The thrust of the argument is that all human experience is part of the larger human condition.

The work that was devoted to this final chapter is obviously a labor of love for Reverend Jordan. The discussions of the combinations of multiculturalism, existentialism and therapy weave their way through comparisons and critiques of various therapeutic approaches. Further exploration is dedicated to how these approaches lend themselves to a philosophical and actual practice of being in the 'here and now'. This concept is rooted in the practice of instilling hope in the belief systems of clients. Reverend Jordan discusses the uniqueness of family structure as a multicultural entity, as well as the development of morals. Each facet of multicultural psychotherapy and existentialism is examined and discussed in a very impassioned, yet realistic manner. Throughout his research Reverend Jordan has addressed the relevance in examining the past in order to better understand the present.

While reading this work the reader is asked to hear Reverend Theodus Jordan passionately explore the vital points of multiculturalism. His research on this daunting topic is focused toward helping the reader comprehend the intricacies and hidden agendas in scholarly works and multicultural practices. The historical significance cannot be ignored. The contemporary context is particularly relevant as our society evolves to allegedly include all our members. Psychotherapy is a very useful tool for the assistance of disenfranchised individuals if practiced with a truly multicultural approach that utilizes an existential model in some form. If this work were a sermon from the pulpit, the listener would be treated to an inspirational, informative experience that is eye-opening and thought provoking. The reader/listener could not help but to become emotionally involved with the work.

It has been my distinct pleasure to assist my dear friend and colleague, Reverend Theodus Jordan in writing this foreword to a very impressive work.

Respectfully: Edward J. McGrath, Ed.D.

PREFACE

THIS INDEPENDENT RESEARCH project known as the IRP, introduces this subject matter for the first time in its present subject matter. The original title "In The Twenty First-Century, Does Multiculturalism Impact Existentialism in Counseling Psychology? If So, How?" puts forth for the first time in a formal sense, the question of how race affects the way we approach psychological and psychotherapeutic counseling here in America.

Most clinicians, doctors, or other health-care providers, enter their own particular codes and ethical standards without ever including the validity of race and how diversity should be treated. Needless to say, traditional psychologists and other practitioners in the therapeutic fields, like their predecessors, fall among two groups: those who treat race and people of color in the traditional "inferior" and "unequal" colonial and pre-colonial period mindset, and those who ignore the race or color of the individual altogether. The sensitive nature of race in any study simply adds too many complications to the study itself, especially when cultures have been divided for centuries based purely along color lines. To this author's knowledge and research, the original title question, "How does Multiculturalism Impact Existentialism in Counseling Psychology?" has never been asked in the context of a formal scientific and intellectual discourse, nor as a *disciplined subject matter.*

There has been very little research done in this area to test the validity or apparatus of a philosophical and a theoretical framework geared especially to test both the *affects* and *effects* of race, color, and racism upon the psyche. The ideological and philosophical thought influential in the earlier part of the 18th and 19th centuries have been driven by the accepted notion of the "inferiority" of the black man vs. the "superiority" of the white man in ordered species, respectively. In Charles Darwin's *Origin of the Species,* Darwin postulated this notion in his "survival of the fittest" nomenclatures where he based his conclusion purely on selected adaptations arranged by himself in hierarchies, which was also hand selected by himself. Later, Sigmund Freud (father of modern-day psychoanalysis) whose only subjects were European whites ignored the question of race, color, and cultural differences altogether.

It is necessary, according to this author, to re-examine both Darwinism and Freudian foundational methodologies to see if there are intricate differences inherent in the psyche of people of color as compared to white individuals' internal and external cultural experience? And to see what significant degrees of differences exist when the above apparatus is applied to multicultural groups and individuals in today's American society; thus, the "Twenty-First Century?" in the title? This author seeks to answer these questions by looking into the history, philosophy, and cultural behavior of the ordinary average everyday mindset as expressed through the conduct of the American conscience through formal counseling and reporting.

The driving forces behind this work and its inquiry have some of its origin in the fact of the fall out or *psychodrama* surrounding the new-age terminology of the word *trauma*, and its sudden rise to fame in this twenty-first century. To be sure, the term itself is not new, but the use and rise of it here, in our new age, has become a potent term when introducing unknown, never-before-seen *behaviors*, which chronicles unknown behavior patterns not yet classified, diagnosed, or normalized. While the medical and psychiatric communities have been thoroughly consumed by this term for centuries, this term *trauma* has yet to be brought to the forefront of scientific-psychological examination, whenever it is suggested as relative to postexilic "Slavery".

In fact, by today's response when it comes to the mentioning of the word *trauma* as related to *Slavery*, it has been one of "forgive and forget," whereas the response to the Holocaust, its impact, its scars, and its lasting effects on its victims of posterity has been one of "never forget"/"never again", lest we allow it to repeat itself. Both "Slavery" and the "Holocaust", respectively, are unforgettable examples whereby the driving forces generated and rooted through these psychic experiences were indeed *traumatic*, yet Slavery has never been treated as a *maladaptive* entity within the scientific community.. . Nor, has "Slavery" ever been adjudicated to the extent that the "Holocaust" has succeeded in the prosecutorial criminality of those still found living and guilty of participating in the atrocities of those events . . . even though "Slavery" happened on American soil while the Holocaust happened on European soil. Yet, the *traumatic* posterity of both crimes still grips both its victims through detrimental affectations of a psychological, sociological, economical, political and painful stigmatization, respectively.

ACKNOWLEDGMENTS

To Tyrone M. Jordan. Thanks for being my son. *I love you!*

THANK YOU, DR. Edward J. McGrath, for the extra mile you went for me to finish this project even when you knew I was lagging behind. You egged me on, not just once but all throughout the Seminar period. *Thank you*! You truly are open minded and one of the good guys!

Thank you, Deana Tassi, for being there for me when I was in pain from a "hate crime." You took my pictures and empathized with me while you were going through your own painful loses. I will never forget you for that. I love you.

Thank you, Rev. Michael Wayne Walker (Pastor, Messiah Baptist Church), for letters of recommendation, which in my mind, helped to get me accepted at Cambridge College. Thank You.

Thanks to Dr. Margaret Howard (administrator/instructor, Tufts' Dental School) for your letter of recommendation. You went that extra mile for me when you really could just have easily said "no". I have admired you for quite some time now. Now I admire you even more. Thank you.

Finally, I thank all my classmates in the Seminar class with Dr. McGrath. You all were very inspirational, each in your own way. Thanks for the ride. It was both exhilarating and illuminating! Very special thanks to Jack Davidson for helping with pagination. Again, I can't thank Dr. McGrath enough for kicking me across the finish line. Many "Hail Maries" to you for never giving up on me. Finally, thanks to Dr. McGrath, for the special *foreword* given to this work and for giving his *credibility* in support of this work. You truly are a very remarkable human being, sir. Thanks!

ABSTRACT STATEMENT

THE PURPOSES OF this independent research project are five reasons. *First,* the author seeks to inject into the world of academia and its curricula a new way of looking at how counseling psychology is approached and defined. *Second,* how multiculturalism impacts existentialism. *Third,* how existentialism influences societies historically and traditionally. *Fourth,* how counseling psychology, multiculturalism, and existentialism will impact America during the twenty-first century and beyond. *Fifth,* to bring attention to the significance and relevance of such a discourse as a discipline worthy of inquiry and deserving of serious discussion that is important and essential in today's world.

The research will delve succinctly into the definition of the three terms and show their relationship with each other, based on the presentation given in the introduction. For example, counseling psychology will be defined first. Then the definition will be further opened to reveal its historical finding, the concept that brought it into being, then there will be an examination of the variegated "psychotherapeutic models," its authors, and founders.

There will be a link showing a deliberate connection of each scientist to Sigmund Freud (1856-1939) and his original psychoanalytical theories and structural models to this scientist's work even though many of these scientists branched into their own specialized fields, developing many and varied models of therapeutic applications. In the chapter on *multiculturalism,* the reader will experience many definitions of this term. There are paradoxes, conflicts, and interchangeable terms used to show multiculturalism's variability. Multiculturalism opens up by attempting to define the word *culture* itself, so that the reader can better grasp this term and see that we all are basically the same underneath our exteriors in terms of what we all value as human beings, no matter the color of our skin, our religions, our languages, our beliefs, our genders, and our creeds.

The next chapter will define existentialism, its origin, its philosophical and theoretical claims and many discourses of thought by those who have tried to make us understand our own lives and our destinies, even when their views reflected or seemed European in nature and background. The final chapter attempts to bring together all three concepts—*counseling psychology, multiculturalism,* and *existentialism*—into a symphony of discipline and discourse for the readers, students, professors, counselors, religious and secular communities . . . as well as for the patients, doctors, and other health-providers, who are involved in the healing of those with mental, physical, emotional, and spiritual brokenness.

STATEMENT OF PURPOSE

THE PURPOSE OF this author's work is to present a **non-Fictional** account of how "counseling-psychology" works within the American psychological community today. Then, this author attempts to show how "counseling psychology" has traditionally presented itself to its American public from a mono-cultural perspective based in a European (white) dialectical context of understanding. This author further attempts to show how the historical affects of "Counseling Psychology" has ignored the "traumatic effects" of slavery's impact upon the average African American or black persons-of-color.

There is the need within this author to state, or restate **unequivocally** that this is a **non-Fictional** treatment of this subject-- "Counseling Psychology". This author's perspective, though it may be novel to most white audiences, conveys factual everyday living experiences and truths to the average African American or Black individual born and living in America today. Why? Because, both the psychological and sociological effects of "slavery's" "stigmatization" and its devastatingly *"traumatic"* experience, has not been medically treated with the scientific apparatus and psychotherapeutic measures as someone, or a family group, who has experienced, or, who has gone through some lesser *traumatic* experience.

Apart from the political, economical, and educational approaches we have witness through the last four decades, *slavery*, with all of its lingering symptoms, maladies, and stigmas, still effectively affects blacks and other persons -of-color with a false-sense of *inferiority*, while it stigmatizes whites with a false-sense of *superiority*, even today. This author believes this is why, the achievement gap will further widen between blacks and whites; why the average income for whites and blacks—both male and female—will continue to be higher among whites than blacks; why there are, and have always been, a higher number of blacks incarcerated than whites historically, why, in employment, hiring, promotions, and better positions will continue to favor whites over blacks; and why, in unemployment, demotions, lack of hiring and firings, and the menial job positions will continue to favor blacks or people -of-color over whites in this 21st. Century as it has for the last twenty Centuries… even before America was a Nation and since it has become a Nation moving toward a "more perfect union".

Such lack in *intervention,* though necessary, has resulted in the continuation and break-down of the mental health of Blacks, Jews, Whites, and persons -of-color, here in America. This is, not even remotely, a healthy society in terms of our deep and varied perspectives, i.e. Blacks, Whites, Jews, Muslims, and other people-of-color—in how we all view the same society, we all live in. The term "equality"—i.e. equal treatment, equal opportunities, equal access, equal justice, and equal protection under the law in much of America lacks credibility even after five centuries of "Democracy"!

The purpose of this work is further demonstrated, by the readings and works of the Pyramid Builders Associate, Inc.—a clinical work-group in Boston (Roxbury) Massachusetts. Here, this health-clinic has been pulled together by a group of dedicated, experienced, and educated black males and their associates to address the problem of *"PTSlaveryD"* or (*Post Traumatic Slavery Disorder*). According to its founders: Omar G. Reid, Psy. D; Sekou Mims, M. Ed., MSW, LCSW; and Larry Higginbottom, MSW, LCSW; says, PTSlaveryD syndrome carries the notion that **"dysfunctional behaviors and disorders that exist among black people have their origins linked to the african slave period".** *
    these authors discuss: "the effects of the intergenerational transmission of slavery's trauma that is exhibited among Black people today from various social and economic classes"*. Their main objectives are:

> ➤ "To understand the origins of PTSlaveryD"
> ➤ "To diagnose individuals suffering from PTSlaveryD";
> ➤ "To identify the symptoms of PTSlaveryD"; and
> ➤ "To be able to use an effective clinical approach to treat the disorder".*

Reid, Mims, and Higginbottoms, gives this author **more** authentication and **more** justification for writing this text. They add **more** validity to this author's argument that there is a need for **"Counseling Psychology"** and a widespread **therapeutic intervention** within *__traumatized__* "Black America".

But at the same time, there is a need for whole America to acknowledge that since the abolishment of *Slavery,* since the theories of *Darwinism,* and now, the influx of *Multiculturalism* throughout America, our entire approach to **"Counseling Psychology"** itself—as a discipline—needs retooling for the 21st. Century. It is from these bases that this work was born. **This is not a fictional work!**

Finally, this book is written for the following audiences: All Libraries in need of a fresh reference book on how America is approaching **"diversity"** in the 21st. Century as *multiculturalism* is exploding. It is also written for physicians and their patients; practitioners and their clients; clinician and their individual and group-subjects; therapist and their subjects; counselors and their subjects; psychiatrist and patients; educators and students; military personnel, colleges, universities, secondary learning situation; religious institutions and secular communities, etc. etc.

- Reference: **PTSlaveryD/Post Traumatic Slavery Disorder: Definition, Diagnosis and Treatment.* By Omar G. Reid, Psy. D; Sekou Mims, M. Ed, MSW; Larry Higginbottom, MSW, LCSW. 2nd. edt. 3rd. prt. (2005).

INTRODUCTION

Does multiculturalism impact existentialism and counseling psychology in the twenty-first century?

THIS AUTHOR FEELS that the answer to the above question is a resounding, *YES!* Throughout this essay, the author will be examining how "counseling psychology", "multiculturalism", and "existentialism", are all intertwined and how these three entities impact each other when it comes to the clinical approach to counseling, in the twenty-first century and beyond.

It is also this author's sole contention and sole belief that psychological counseling today has shifted greatly and fundamental in terms of how psychologists view original theories and have applied these theories in their approaches to their clients in the past; but, given the highly multicultural influx and diversity in this new American milieu, how those original theories would contrast in counseling psychology's approach today? Not only is this true based on the geographical migration of other cultures moving into America, but also due to the internal integration and amalgamation of other cultures infiltrating into what has often been a monolithic white-dominated culture, which has been the model or the paradigm of cultural expression, traditionally, in America since America began—the doctor/patient relationship. This question has plagued this writer for quite some time now, even before coming into the Counseling Psychology Program. Since learning some basic phenomena in the understanding of human psychological development and gaining some small insights into the personality within my own social construct, analytically, this writer now feels compelled to examine up close and personal certain fundamental and theoretical concepts.

The writer's approach is to use interdisciplinary studies to show a commonality of his theme imbedded already within the fabric of knowledge common to the well-informed community in which we live today. That is, historical, philosophical, psychological, ecological, economical, political, educational, and environmental approaches to show how these disciplines are interacting with cultural development; how these are interrelated in such a way that causes, affects, influences, and contributes to societal growth or societal denigration amid its racial and psychological actors. The writer, by shedding light or giving clear and convincing evidence through this work, concludes that the above subject is a viable and relevant issue. This work will give to us—counselors and educators—more insight into how we affect and impact one another as individuals as we interact both within our domains and outside of our domains, no matter which format such interactions take on. This is especially true in the counselor/client or the doctor/patient relationship.

This writer's essential motivational approach is imbedded in what Irvin D. Yalom, an existentialist himself, has called in his book, the "gift of therapy," the "here-and-now experience;" the "major thrust of therapeutic power," etc. In other words, the day-to-day, face to-face, interactions and activities of human behavior. The play-by-play, whether verbal or non-verbal behaviors—including gestures, kinesthetic energy, and other body languages that communicate one's inner feelings . . . Yalom's use of the "here-and-now" points to the therapist ability to keep himself as well as the client, "in the present" as they interact in their dance toward healing (Yalom 2002).

This writer uses the "here-and-now" to establish authenticity as the basis for his rational validity in writing on this subject matter. The "here-and-now" of the writer's experience provides the social microcosm and scope of vision needed to show the inherent creative power held within this writer which compels him to pursue this subject matter. The author's strategic plan for attacking this subject matter will be one of discovery. (The author, the writer, this work—all terms that will be used interchangeably throughout the body of this work) most assuredly brings to this work certain preconceived thoughts, theorems, assumptions, hypothesis, notions, axioms, beliefs, and own experiences both psychologically and sociologically developed while living in this American macrocosm. However, this author will be true and stick to the forum of his own experiential discoveries.

Definitions:

THEODUS JORDAN

The first task is to define the three most important operating terms in our title, which is *multiculturalism*; *existentialism*; and *counseling psychology* beginning with counseling psychology, and working our way through existentialism, then finally to multiculturalism for purposes of continuity and fluidity in thought.

First, this writer feels it necessary to divide the term *counseling psychology* into a single-word definition, and then combine these two terms into a single meaning for a quicker grasp of this writer's work, since the school catalogue really did not define this word as a single term. It does, however, give an operational definition of *counseling* in the *Introduction Course Manual CCP501*, as taught by Professor Jeanne Richardson.

Professor Richardson gives an operational definition of her *counseling course* which fits this writer's purpose fully. She writes: "Counseling combines assessment, learning resources, cultural and racial factors, <u>roles</u> on the interdisciplinary team, elements of professional training, professional issues (including ethics and relevant laws), credentialing, professional associations, making the best use of supervision and consultation, supervisor and agency expectation, ground rules, resources and responsibilities which are associated with the master's level training in counseling." (Richardson 2005)

In the Cambridge College Academic Catalogue 2004-2005 Psychology was given a definition under the banner of Systems Thinking (PSY110). It provides the operational definition this writer needs in making his case, which was sourced from the *Concise Columbia Encyclopedia*. It states: "System thinking psychology introduces a theoretical approach for understanding the relationships and interactions of individuals, families, groups, and organizations. Much attention is paid to application of the systemic model and how it differs from the linear model, when studying human interactions, or analyzing social problems, and developing interventions. Students apply systems theory [psychology] to problems [as] they select from their daily lives or jobs." The word *psychology* in its original sense means "the science of human behavior." (1983)

The writer firmly believes that the term *system* makes for a more operational term which is more useful and more relational in the task of completing this work. So then, by combining both these terms—counseling psychology—the writer now has the tools he needs to build a frame by which to hang his theories onto to show how multiculturalism affects (impacts) existentialism and the way we approach counseling in the twenty-first century, as opposed to how counseling was conducted or applied earlier on in American society. But before we go on, there is still the task of defining multiculturalism and existentialism.

Multiculturalism is defined as: "The belief that a society should respect and promote all the various cultures or ethnic groups of which it is composed."(*The American Heritage Dictionary, 2nd Edition*, ed. Boyer/Devinne/Harris/Soukhnov/Steinhardt, 1991)

This definition directly fits this writer's theories, concepts, and ideas of how this term, *multiculturalism*, is explored throughout the duration of this work. In fact, this definition underlies this author's reasons for wanting to expose this subject matter.

The term *multiculturalism* will be used interchangeably with the following: diversity, cultural pluralism, sub-groups and combined subgroups. The idea is to dispel any notion of exclusion of any group or individuals, who thrive here in America—whether legally, naturalized, or natively born—as un-American, or *persona non grata*. In this work, all Americans are considered hyphenated (i.e. Afro-American; Euro-American; Asian-American; Latin-American; etc.) . . .notwithstanding of course, the Native Americans. (Naylor 1997)

In defining *existentialism*, this author looks at both the earlier European view and early American view of this term. First, the early European views: Two basic views emerged earlier on because of a philosophical movement which challenged the essentialism of existence. Existence is from the Latin roots *ex* and *sistere*, which means to step forth or emerge. (Reese 1980)

The philosophical analysis of the concept of existence is in some respects similar to the analysis of the concept of matter, according to the *Dictionary of Philosophy and Religion*, as "matter" stands in contrast to "form," so "existence" stands in contrast to "essence." And since mental activity is concerned with the characteristics of things, the latter terms, 'forms' and 'essence' seems less puzzling than "matter" and "existence." He goes on to say, if "existence" cannot be characterized, how is one to discuss it? And, if it can be characterized, how does it stand in contrast to "essence?" (Reese 1980)

As results of this movement, i.e. on *essentialism* and *existence*, concentration shifted mainly on the human condition. When it came to humanity, two views of man emerged: (1) man's view as subjected to a spiritual God, i.e. Theistic; and (2) man's view of himself as self-existing, i.e. Atheistic. While earlier philosophers from Plato, Aristotle, then much later, Thomas Aquinas, Duns Scotus, Immanuel Kant, Hegel, kierkegaard, Brentano, Husserl, Bertrand Russell, Heidegger, Weiss, Sartre, and Quine, Nietzsche, Unamuno, Ortega, Jaspers, and (Theologians) Bultmann, Marcel, Paul Tillich, and others, have all distinguished themselves in the discussion of "existentialism." (Reese 1980)

They have all fallen among either the atheistic views of Nietzsche and/ or the theistic views led by kierkegaard. Briefly: Friedrich Nietzsche was born in Rockne, Prussia. Although he was a brilliant student in his earlier years, he spent the last eleven years of his life being insane. However, earlier, he became a professor of major proportions. He developed the "God is Dead" doctrine and believed that each individual must seek his own values, providing a bridge to their future, thus, his atheistic views flourished; and such was his existential beliefs. (Nietzsche 1997)

Soren Kierkegaard was a Danish philosopher and theologian. He was born in Copenhagen. He challenged the Hegelian (Dialectical) philosophy, thus substituting and replacing essentialism. kierkegaard emphasized the individual component as "essential but the importance of subjectivity, and Angst or anguish, as the central emotion of human life." With respect to God, he stressed the need for a "leap of faith." (Reese 1980)

In the following chapters, Nietzsche and kierkegaard were the two primary ruling views of philosophical thought at the turn of the nineteenth century. This author will examine how the concept of existentialism laid down in its original and basic foundational schools of thought by these philosophers and others, is impacted by multiculturalism in today's society as we apply counseling psychology by today's standards, in the twenty-first century.

In chapter one, the author will more fully define counseling psychology, psychopathology, and psychotherapy and how multiculturalism is approached in today's clinical situations both as an individual and in group dynamics. In chapter two, the author will examine the term *culture*, and fully explore and fully explore its basic meaning, concept, and relationship to multiculturalism.

In chapter three, psychopathology will be explored to see how psychopathological traits are derived from the existentialism of our daily lives. Also, the author will show how existentialism is inextricably connected to cultures and individuals within those cultures. In chapter four, the author will answer the questions: What are the issues that are driving this work, i.e., counseling psychology/multiculturalism/existentialism? Why do these issues matter, in today's society? Why are these issues relevant or important to this author, the field of counseling psychology, and to the larger society? Also, in this chapter, the author will connect the three modalities of counseling psychology, existentialism, and multiculturalism, into a discipline of study, as the contribution and purpose of doing this work is revealed. And finally, this author will show his methodology used in presenting how counseling psychology, multiculturalism, and existentialism, will thrive into the twenty-first century and beyond. A conclusion and an appendix will follow, pulling together all aspects of this work and its essential theme.

CHAPTER 1

Definitions

A N OVERVIEW OF counseling psychology is the purpose of this chapter. The purpose of this work in counseling psychology is to understand how diversity in our present milieu (existential experience) impacts the way, in which, we as practitioners engage in the healing process of our forever evolving clientele in today's society.

This work assumes the validity of the claim that diversity impacts counseling psychology, especially in counseling methodologies which have been handed down historically, and through scientific discovery for more than fifty years now—especially the Sigmund Freud (b.1856-d.1939), model of psychoanalysis which seems to be the very foundational model which most psychologist and psychotherapist are founded upon in contemporary society. The term *psychotherapy*, though not coined by Freud himself, was nevertheless in the making when most of his students and colleagues were both adapting and parting from his model of sexual-gratification forming their own variations of the theories of Freud. Authors Raymond J. Corsini, PhD, University of Hawaii (Honolulu), and Danny Wedding, PhD, MPH, director at the Missouri Institute of Mental Health, of St. Louis, Missouri, have written a text entitled *Current Psychotherapies, 7ʰ Edition*. (Corsini/ Wedding 2005)

In it, Corsini introduces the text by defining psychotherapy. He gives a very comprehensive definition which says:

> Psychotherapy is a formal process of interaction between two parties. Each party usually consisting of one person but with the possibility that there maybe two or more people in each party for the purpose of amelioration of distress in one of the two parties relative to any or all of the following areas of disability: malfunctions or cognitive functions (disorders of thinking),

affective functions (suffering or emotional discomforts) or behavioral functions (inadequacy of behavior) with the therapist having some theory of personality's origins, development, maintenance and change along with some method of treatment logically related to the theory and professional and legal approval to act as a therapist.

While the above definition by Corsini is somewhat lengthy, it does seem to encapsulate the whole idea of psychotherapy with all of its many approaches and newer techniques of therapeutic innovations. At least it does for this author's purpose for both writing on this subject matter and for the readers to have some understanding of how the terms—counseling psychology, psychotherapy/psychotherapist, and psychologist are used throughout this thesis. Perhaps then, the best view that this author can give in order to bring about both substance and clarity to this subject matter is to say that these terms are to be used almost interchangeably. (Corsini 2005)

The terms *counseling* and *psychotherapy* are in fact two different words when used properly. Terms, which are interchangeable when used as instruments to direct, lead, promote, indicate, facilitate, admonish, advice, steer, and drive individual clients who have expressed a problem of inability in coping with life to seek help. By seeking help and healing from someone considered to have the ability to do so, or someone considered to be an expert relative to a client's special need. (Corsini 2005)

There are some subtle differences in the terms, however, which are a lot less subtle in terms of the outcome and results of treatment applied. According to Corsini/Wedding, "counseling is problem-oriented, while psychotherapy is more person-oriented. While the actual processes that occur in counseling and psychotherapy are identical they do differ relative to the time spent [duration of the process]." (Horney 1942)

Again the term *counseling* works inside all modes of psychotherapeutic applications trying to help people improve themselves through symbolic methods. Thus the terms *counseling* and *psychotherapy* are the instruments by which therapy is conducted in any session. These determine the interaction of the relationship imposed when the therapist/counselor, meets the patient/client. (Painter 1981)

Here in this threshold, total strangers come together to search for newer horizons, which for the client/patient, hopefully, opens the pathways of self and inner discoveries that ultimately leads to fulfillment and wholeness. But for the counselor/therapist, another opportunity to use his/her vast skills, knowledge, experience, and abilities to procreate wellness to others and further advance and broaden the field of counseling psychology opening up newer and vast vistas, spreading what Irvin D. Yalom, MD, has called the gift of therapy. (Yalom 2003)

Relevance?

As this author has stated briefly above, counseling psychology, as with all psychologies, psychotherapies, psychiatry, has its origin in the psychoanalytic theories of Sigmund Freud and his contemporaries. Even though psychoanalysis is Freud's personal discoveries and methodology, it was also his major psychoanalytical technique. Freud's interaction with his patient approach has been the basic form used by his followers, critics, and those who have long since parted completely from his theories. (Freud 1901)

Yet in a real sense, his approach is the underpinning structure in counseling psychology used by all other therapist and psychotherapist interacting with—whether it is, one patient, two patients, or in group dynamics. It is important to say that the similarities both start and stop here as far as theories, ideologies, methodologies, approaches, formats, and the applications of the various methods used as developed by many other social-scientists, psychotherapists, psychoanalysts, doctors, psychiatrist, and other counselors as, being simply, prototypes of Freud. (Freud 1914a)

These contemporaries, colleagues, descendants, and progenitors all have totally established and distinguished themselves through their own works. The point here being, that counseling psychology, in today's society, as experts use and apply their own uniquely developed psychotherapeutic approaches, had its origin in the methodologies as well as therapeutic methods and application of Freud's structured interactive handling of his patients. (Corsini, Wedding, and Jones 1953) Jacob A. Arlow (Wedding/Corsini, 2005), a psychoanalyst himself, makes the following statement in his text which support this author's claims about Freud: {Paraphrased}

> Psychoanalysis is a system of psychology derived from the discoveries of Sigmund Freud. It was originally used by Freud for the treatment of hysteria. Psychoanalysis is now used to treat many other psychological difficulties, and is the foundation for a general theory of psychology. Knowledge derived from the treatment of individual patients has led to insights into art, religion, social organization, child development, and education. In addition, by elucidating the influence of unconscious forces on the physiology of the body, psychoanalysis has made it possible to understand and treat many psychosomatic illnesses. (Arlow 1963) (Corsini and Wedding 2005; Arlow1989)

As a scholar in psychoanalytical theory and psychotherapy, Arlow believed, as this author agrees, that modern-day psychological systems, including *counseling psychology*, have its origin as a result of Freud's work universally. (Arlow 1988)

This of course means that Freud's psychoanalysis has already influenced many forms of modern psychotherapies such as the Adlerian psychotherapy, which emphasizes "holism as opposed to reductionism occurring in any social context." According to Harold H. Mosak of the Corsini and Wedding on *Current Psychotherapies*, Alfred Adler (1870-1937) called individual psychology as such that "views the person holistically as creative, responsible, 'becoming' individual moving toward fictional goals within his or her phenomenal field. It holds that one's lifestyle is sometimes self-defeating because of inferiority feelings." (2005; Adler 1931, 1958)

The individual with psychopathological feelings is discouraged rather than sick, and the therapeutic task is to encourage the person to activate his or her social interest and to develop a new lifestyle through relationship, analysis, and action methods. Adlerian, though later parted from Freud, constantly reminded his colleagues of how he had begun under the influence and tutelage of Freud.

Adler parted with Freud in later years because of Freud's emphasis on the role of psychosexual development and the now famous Oedipus complex and Electra complex. Both of which dominated all of Freud's theoretical constructs. Adler chose to focus on "the effects of children's perceptions of their family constellation and their struggle to find a {secured} place of significance within their family." (Adler 1969)

The Analytical Psychotherapy of Carl Gustav Jung (1875-1961), written by psychoanalyst Claire Douglas (1957), is based on Jung's analytical psychology of the human personality where Jung puts forth his own "psychodynamic system, building upon Freud's and Adler's perspectives, but offering an expanded view of the human personality and its collective realities."

Again, Jung's model presents the human psyche in a map format which encompasses both conscious and unconscious elements, including both a transpersonal (archetypal) and personal layer in the unconscious. The goals of the psychotherapist here are for the reintegration, self-knowledge, and individuation, with a heartfelt awareness of the human condition, individual responsibility, and a connection to transcendence, thereby, replacing a wounded, one-sided, rationalistic, and limited sense of self. (Jung 1935, 1966)

In understanding Jung, there are four basic terms: (1) psyche—defined as the combination of spirit, soul, idea; (2) *psyche* reality—was viewed as the sum of both conscious and unconscious in process; (3) collective unconscious—term used for the vast, hidden psychic resource shared by all human being; and (4) archetype—is an organizing principle, a system of readiness, and a dynamic nucleus of energy. Jung, like Adler, though highly influenced, finally broke with Freud over his form of psychoanalysis. (Jung 1929, 1933, 1961)

The Person-Centered Therapy Developed by Carl R. Rogers (1902-1987), written by Nathaniel J. Raskin and Carl Rogers (1959), is known today as Rogerian. The Rogerian-therapeutic approach is based upon a phenomenological view of human life and helping relationships . . . . A self-directed growth process which follows the Provision and reception of a particular kind of relationship characterized by genuineness, nonjudgmental caring, and empathy.

According to Rogers (1986), "the most fundamental and pervasive concept in client-centered therapy is trust." Furthermore Rogers believed that there is an actualizing tendency present in all humans and all living organisms (and inanimate objects such as the stars, crystals, etc.) moving toward the realization of full potential. He called this actualizing force the formative tendency.

In application, the therapist must be able to "trust in the client's innate capacity for growth." He/she must learn to be disciplined enough and strong enough "to learn to follow the client's lead and to and to do nothing that might disempowered the self-directing client . . . because the valuing of the client's inalienable right to self-determination permeates the person-centered approach to therapy and had been described as the non-directive attitude." Carl Ransom Rogers-Freudian connection was made at the Teacher's College of Columbia University. (Rogers 1986b)

Albert Ellis in the 1950s developed his method of psychotherapy known as rational emotive behavioral therapy (REBT). Ellis, a trained clinical psychologist, "held that when a highly charged emotional consequence (C) follows a significant activating event (A), A may seem to, but actually does not cause C. Instead, claims Ellis, emotional consequences are largely created by B—the individual's belief system. Whenever an undesirable emotional consequence occurs, such as severe anxiety, this usually involves the person's irrational belief, and when these beliefs are effectively disputed (at point D), challenging them rationally and behaviorally, the disturbed consequences are reduced. (2004)

According to Ellis (1997), REBT has integrated and viewed cognition and emotion—thought, feeling, desires, and action—as interacting with each other, from the inception of his therapeutic method. He believes that his model is a comprehensive cognitive-affective behavioral theory and practice of psychotherapy. REBT is both minds and body, or of thinking/ feeling/ wanting (contents of the mind) and behavior (contents of the body). REBT theory further states that humans rarely change a profound self-defeating belief unless they act against it.

Taken such an action is the core of understanding what REBT therapy does . . . it helps to bring the individual, who is seeking relief, face to face with both the rational (the constructive self) as well as the irrational (the defeating self). Because everyone has these competing two-selves competing simultaneously, the effective therapist helps the individual by helping him/ her to recognize these opposing selves, then allying with him/her to help defeat the irrational self-defeating domination. Ellis is connected to Freud by contradistinction. (Ellis 1998)

Behavior therapy did not arrive on the scene until the 1950s as psychotherapy. It was defined as the application of modern learning theory to the treatment of clinical problems, according to G. Terrence Wilson, a clinical psychologist and writer. He says the phrase *modern learning theory* refers to the principles and procedures of classical and operant conditioning. (B.F. Skinner 1953; Wolfe 1960)

Behavior therapy as it expands is marked by diversity of views and has a tendency to overlap other psychotherapeutic approaches. The three main approaches in contemporary behavior therapy include (1) applied behavior analysis, (2) a neo-behaviorist meditational stimulus-response model, and (3) social-cognitive theory.

B.F. Skinner (1953) is credited with the applied behavioral analysis model. He believed that behavior is operationally based on the stimuli it receives, i.e., behavior is a function of its consequences. Thus treatment procedures are based on altering relationships between the overt behaviors and their consequences. (Skinner 1953)

The neo-behaviorist mediation stimulus-response (S-R) model came from the learning theories of Ivan Pavlov, E.R. Guthrie, Clark Hull, O.H. Mowrer, and N.E. Miller. Unlike the operant approach, says Wilson, the S-R model is meditational, with intervening variables and hypothetical constructs prominently featured. The S-R theorists are interested particular in anxieties. (Bandura 1969)

The social-cognitive theory approach itself is based on three separate yet interacting regulatory systems which are called (1) external stimulus events, (2) external reinforcement, and (3) cognitive meditational processes, says Dr. Albert Bandura of the University Akron, Ohio. Bandura explains, "personal and environmental factors do not function as independent determinants rather, they determine each other." (Bandura 1977)

The basic assumption here, according to Bandura, is not so much experience itself, but rather the person's interpretation of that experience, which produces psychological disturbance. Today behavioral therapy is commonly referred to as CBT (cognitive behavior therapy). Bandura and the behavioral therapy are connected to Freud through the works and influence of Albert Ellis, who was influenced by Alfred Adler, who was directly influenced by Freud's clinical approach.

Aaron T. Beck, a PhD at the University of Pennsylvania, in describing cognitive therapy, said it is based on a theory of personality which maintains that people respond to life events through a combination of cognitive affective, motivational, and behavioral responses. These responses are based in human evolution and individual learning history. (2002)

The cognitive system deals with the way that individuals perceive, interpret, and assign meanings to events. It interacts with the other affective, motivational, and physiological systems to process information from the physical and social environments, and to respond accordingly. Sometimes responses are maladaptive because of misperceptions or dysfunctional, idiosyncratic interpretations of situations. Beck (1979) contends that cognitive therapy aims to adjust information processing and initiate positive change in all systems by acting through the cognitive system. In a collaborative process, the therapist and patient examine the patient's beliefs about himself, other people, and the world. The patient's maladaptive conclusions are treated as testable hypotheses.

In short, cognitive therapy can be called a theory, a system of strategies, and a series of techniques. Each system is involved in a struggle for survival— cognitive, behavioral, affective, and motivational. The counselor, therapist, or psychotherapist, strategy here is to develop a collaborative enterprise between himself and the patient, explore dysfunctional interpretations, and try to modify these dysfunctions. (Beck 2003)

Albert Ellis, the behavioral therapist above, was a powerful influence on Beck. Both gave major credits to the development of cognitive behavioral therapy. Ellis, however, confronted the patients with their personal philosophies to show them as unrealities. Beck, on the other hand, made the patient a collaborator that causes him/her to do research to verify their realities or not. Immanuel kant and Sigmund Freud in their structural theory and dept psychologies were major influences of Beck. (Beck 1985)

The existential psychotherapy, according to Rollo May, PhD, and Irvin Yalom, MD, and existentialists trained in psychiatry, said that existential psychotherapy arose in the early 1940s and 50s as a result of the frustrations and dissatisfactions of the scientific communities in European models based solely on Sigmund Freud and Carl Jung. Their frustrations were over the lack of the scientific communities concern with "finding a way of understanding human beings that was more reliable and more basic than the current psychotherapies." (May 1961)

These new existentialists like May and Yalom, began to ask such questions, like "are we seeing patients as they really are, or are we seeing a projection of our theories about them?" Yalom and May go on to explain that existential psychotherapy does not present any new set of rules for therapy, but ask deep questions about the nature of the human being and the nature of anxiety, despair, grief, loneliness, isolation, and anomie. It also deals centrally with the questions of creativity and love. (May 1958)

Paradoxes:

The job of the counseling psychologist in this situation is to understand the meaning of these human experiences, devise methods of therapy that help the individual and not destroy the individual. May's connection to Freud was influenced when he attended the neo-Freudian institute in New York around the 1950s. (May 1981; Yalom 1981)

The Gestalt therapy was founded by Frederick "Fritz" Perls. The counseling psychologist's task here is "to synthesize various cultural and intellectual trends in the 1940s and 50s into a new gestalt, one that provided a sophisticated clinical and theoretical alternative to the two other main theories of their day: behaviorism and classical psychoanalysis." (1973, 1976)

Gestalt therapy started "as a revision of psychoanalysis by Perls, in 1942-1992 and developed as a wholly independent, integrated system." Gestalt therapy is an experiential and humanistic approach; it works with patients' awareness and awareness skills rather than using the classic psychoanalytic reliance on the analyst's interpretation of the unconscious." (1992)

The gestalt therapist is engaged with their patients and frequently discloses his or her own experience, both experience of the moment in the therapy hour and life experience, in a relationship based on mutuality. Fritz was related to Freud by revolutionizing the basic ideas that Freud brought to the Western culture. (1942; 1992)

Arnold A. Lazarus (1976) developed the multimodal therapy technique. It is a systematic and comprehensive psychotherapeutic approach. A basic premise is that patients are usually troubled by a multitude of specific problems that should be dealt with by a broad range of specific methods. A multimodal assessment examination would consist of the following formula called BASIC ID. Each letter represents one category of an assessment. For example, B=Behavior; A=Affect, S=Sensation, I=Imagery, C=Cognition, I=Interpersonal Relationships, and D=Drugs/Biology.

These provide the counseling therapist with the tools to isolate or separate specific problems in an operational way and answer the question for each client upon complete scrutiny: What works? For Whom? Under which conditions? Lazarus is tied to Freud's influence, because of his earlier education in the 1950s at the University of Witwatersrand in Johannesburg, South Africa, where the psychotherapeutic climate there was predominantly Freudian and Rogerian. (Lazarus 1989)

The family therapist is bombarded with both theory and applying treatment methods consistently and at all times during the intervention of family therapy once therapy has begun. Irene and Herbert Goldenberg, the family therapist team, has said, "family therapy represents a form of intervention in which members of a family are assisted to identify and change problematic, maladaptive, self-defeating, repetitive relationship patterns." (Whitaker 1988)

Family therapy is unlike individual-focused therapy because in family therapy the identified patient (the family member who is considered the problem) is also viewed as the symptom bearer, expressing the family's disequilibrium of current dysfunction. The family system itself is treated as the primary unit of treatment and not the identified patient. The symptomatic behaviors in neurotic individuals were the earlier influences for family psychotherapists as they are known today. (Goldenberg 2004)

According to Jacob L. Moreno (1889-1974), psychodrama therapy was developed early in the 1930s. It was mainly for groups, but when modified can be applied with family therapy and with individuals. It draws on natural capacity for imaginative, make-believe play that is evident in childhood. In adulthood, this capacity is used in a more focused, task-oriented ways, for example, a candidate rehearsing for a political office. (Moreno 1946, 1969)

The psychodrama methods may also be used to clarify the dynamics of relationships in group therapy. The therapist or counseling psychologist's task here is to invite a client to role-play some aspect of the client's problem, and then the therapist uses psycho dramatic techniques to draw the client out. Moreno (1999) was forced to move to the United States in 1925 because of postwar hardship in Europe. Once here, Freud's influence was so evident early in the nineteenth century, he had to have felt it.

Experiential psychotherapy as a concept is a model of usefulness rather than a theory of truth, according to its author and founder Alvin R. Mahrer. New, Mahrer says, experiential psychotherapy is based largely upon "philosophy of science and existential philosophy." Its conceptual system, aims, and goals can be thought of as a substantial departure from previous thought in both the field of psychology and the field of psychotherapy.

The psychotherapist or counselor, has two goals in every session: (1) to enable the person to undergo a radical, deep-seated, transformational change into becoming the person that he or she is capable of becoming; and (2) for the person to become essentially free of whatever painful feelings and situations are front and center for the person during each session. (Mahrer 2000a)

Mahrer (2001b) is connected to Freud through the influence of Carl Rogers, who had done parallel work in experiential therapy. Also the works of Carl Whitaker and John Warkentin and others helped to coin the term *experiential psychology.*

Dialectical behavioral therapy (DBT), in theory, according to Paul Gerson, PhD, Licensed Psychologist/CAGS of Cambridge College, is built on the method of Hegel and Plato's model of dialectical revolution. That is, a method of logic or argumentation done by disclosing the contradictions (antithesis) in an opponent's argument (thesis) and overcoming it by a solution called a (synthesis). (Gerson 2005; workshop)

The behavioral therapist emphasis here is upon change, problem solving, rationality, logic, and experimenting. Radical acceptance is freedom from suffering, according to Professor Gerson. DBT correlates to the Zen model of acceptance. The idea of DBT, however, concludes with recognizing one's maladaptive behavior and acting in ways to improve it by opposite behavior to it or increasing positive behaviors which reinforces the desired behavior. The therapist's task or the counseling psychologist's task is to help provide guidance and techniques to accomplish the goal behavior.

Summary:

The above overview of counseling psychology, its history and background, should serve as the foundation and definition needed in order to establish the nature and value of the subject matter as a discipline. And how it is used or applied to all ethnic groups residing throughout this America.

Today the common thread as shown in each psychotherapeutic example above is linked to the Freudian construct as far as the overall approach and content on how we conduct therapy here in America. Yet society today models only one single construct in its counseling approached. That one approach still lies within the Freudian mold of how mental illness and counseling psychology, as well as psychotherapy, is applied in today's society. This one model or one construct, has been both monolithic and/ or monotype.

There has to be a new approach in how counseling psychology treats its clients today. The following are just some of the reasons, but only the obvious ones. First, since Sigmund Freud, the founder of modern-day psychoanalysis, the world has evolved from an agricultural and industrial society to an informational and service production society. Second, computers and technology have replaced time and distance both geographically and socially . . . causing greater autonomy in the exchange of knowledge, ideas, and truths—both basic and fundamental to the original American colonialist constructed idealism. There have also been new and different cultural explosions altering the single white European model of the Imperialistic clientele. (Nevins, Commager 1962)

These new and different experiences have profoundly disturbed and shaken the very depths of our human nature, moving this generation beyond the scope and vision of Freud, and others of his time. Though we all are possessed with human emotions, because of our human nature—no matter what the generational grouping we live within—we are still locked into our humanity.

As human beings, we have a gamut of human emotions forever intergraded into our human system—all of us—responding to our human conditions, both from within and from without. It is through our human emotions, such responses are communicated to the environment in which each of us live. Each of us, however, has the same strand of human emotions. We will respond differently to those emotions at any given time. (Puner 1961)

The third reason why there must be more than one approach to counseling psychology in today's society has to do with Sigmund Freud himself, who is called the father of psychoanalysis. Fundamentally, the context and structure by which he has developed and evolved makes him, in this author's mind, both hero and villain at the same time.

Helen Walker Puner, foreword by Erich Fromm, in her book entitled *Freud, His Life and His Mind* (1961), explains, "Like any other person, he can only be understood in light of his humanity including his frailties and his brilliance. The man who fathered the ideas, which have proven to be so significant for our time, was at bottom as fallible and frail as other men."

This author agrees that no matter how brilliant one becomes by his driven interest, he is still locked into his humanity and does not evolve into infallibility. He simply stays a human being. As human beings, we continued to evolve. Freud was no more, or no less, different. In fact, at the time he began—born 1856, died 1939—Darwinism had been accepted and widely circulated as dominant and leading themes and thought of that day. Freud himself entered college to study biology, expecting a career to explore the physiological inferiority of human kind started by Darwinism many years before. (Levey, Greenhall 1983). This is why much of Freud's earlier works reflect models borrowed from physics and chemistry. He was influenced by Darwinism and the imperialism of his day.

Freud was therefore, socialized and cultivated, molded, and profoundly impacted by the influences of his surroundings just as any young person would have been. He, as did many (white) thinkers of his time, believed in the inferiority of the black man (Negro). More specifically, slavery as an institution, and the "inferiority" of the "black man" was a well-known and established ideological concept in colonialism, as imperialism gripped Europe and prevailed in Freud's time. This was part of the reality of his experience.

This included the Nazism in Germany. These paradoxes further presented Freud (of Jewish descent) as others before him (Abraham Lincoln as well) with a constant and nagging dilemma concerning their own personal freedoms as how to go about keeping others in bondage based on the concept, or the autonomous notion that some humans are inferior by birth based solely on their skin color and natural bestiality. Whites were superior however, based on the virtue of their white skin.

It is in this context that Freud's and others' (Western thinkers) minds have been shaped by these social psychological patterns. For these and other reasons are why today's approach to counseling psychology needs intervention and retooling. A fourth and final reason is multiculturalism itself; which brings us to chapter two of this work.

CHAPTER 2

Multiculturalism
(A Functional Definition)

B EFORE WE CAN talk about multiculturalism, first the author must define the word *culture* itself and how it will be used throughout this chapter. When defining the word *culture* there must be a context from which it is developed. No cultures exist outside a context, experience, or social construct. All cultures evolve from a social construct and a social contextual experience. (A. Kroeber and C. Kluckhohn 1952)

According to these two leading scholars in the field of anthropology, the most difficult problem to overcome is defining culture. In fact, these authors sought to define the word *culture* by listing terms associated with social structures or social organizations and fitting them onto a visible model to show the many ways culture is defined by our society from the laymen view point.

For example, the authors above suggest that there are eight approaches to defining the concept of culture: (1) Historical—this refers to a social heritage (tradition) passed on from generation to generation. (2) Behavioral—whereas culture is seen or viewed as shared and learned human behavior, usually meaning a way of life. (3) Normative—which equates culture with ideas, values, rules, for living. (4) Functional—a definition that sees culture as the way humans solve problems in adapting to the environment. (5) Mental constructive—complex of ideas or learned habits that inhibit impulses and distinguish human from animals. (6) Structural—sees culture as patterned and interrelated ideas, symbols or behaviors. (7) Symbolic interpretations see culture as assigning arbitrary meaning that is shared in a society. (8) Social process—takes into account social, moral, and political consequences. (kroeber, kluckhohn 1952)

Another team of scholars, Fredrick Gamst and Edward Norbeck (1976), has characterized culture as "the human ways of maintaining life and perpetuating the species, a system of learned socially transmitted pattern of ideas, sentiments, social arrangements, and objects tied to the symbols created and used to refer to them. Culture comes from commonality, as something taught, learned and shared in groups (some big and some small) that helps human adapt to both the natural environments and the socio-cultural environments humans create."

However, this author's work is not about authenticating culture; this author accepts the validity of all cultures known to man. This work is about the combinations of cultures coming together to form multicultural societies, and the psychological framework by which those within societies are influenced and will thrive. (Spradley, McCurdy 1972)

A third and vital point about why this author needs to define *culture* has to do with how to distinguish those aspects of culture which both dominate and reduce societies into visible models that show how the society really functions as opposed to how it claims it is functioning.

Here, with this somewhat bereft overview of the word *culture*, we can now move to reconnect the prefix *multi*—to the word *culture* (multicultural). Thus the author now can proceed with his original subject matter of multiculturalism as it is related to counseling psychology and existentialism.

Multiculturalism (relevance to the theme)

Multiculturalism has come to be the symbol, and in some ways, the test or the barometer for measuring democracy in America today. How far have we come in our own experiment into democracy? That is, society's right of all cultures to have equal rights, equal access, voice, equal opportunity, chance, a level playing field, equal distribution of revenues, and equal distribution of jobs for employment (a job of your qualifications). Education should be demanded and paid for by society as a whole—regardless of affordability—because it is vital to any democracy. Health-care system (not welfare as we have known it); but as social security blanket, like jobs, and the right to an education, that insures both our daily existence as a nation and a future for our children, all children, in a free, responsible, and liberated society. (Barrett 1984)

Multiculturalism is also denied and objected to by some as invalid or unnecessary terminology. Multiculturalism does not necessarily imply that a culture has automatically assimilated into another culture or a larger culture. Many societies just try to ignore differences but such societies are proving, even today, that human beings are not to be ignored, simply because one part is rich, and the other part made poor by the same set of circumstances seen through two different perspectives. (Havilland 1997)

While multiculturalism is truly an attempt to alleviate differences brought by racism, sexism, anti-Semitism, religions, languages, appearances, creeds, and color-of-skin (including hues), elitism, class, and poverty, multiculturalism's goal has become a two-fold mission. First, as a tool or remedy, multiculturalism can begin to annihilate myths, long-held prejudices, fears and start to penetrate the "superiority complex" now held by a large majority of the monolithic/monotype main stream Americans (Gamst, Norbeck 1976).

The second mission of multiculturalism is to find both harmony and look for the balance between each race while we are learning to respect and applaud our diversities (differences) that we are also learning to acknowledge and to embrace our similarities. Like our diversities, our similarities are interwoven into our humanity. Like all things physical, mental, natural, spiritual, temporal, material, ephemeral, inanimate, and human, this is the nature of being. (Crunden 1994)

Multiculturalism is the object of intense debate today. This author believes that the underlining issue being talked about, whether it is politics, race, political correctness, curriculum, the allocation of federal dollars, the hiring practices in today's markets and corporations, or intense debate from the right or left, it is clear that diversity—multiculturalism—is the driving force of the day. It is here that the plot is beginning to thicken—in our racial and ethnic diversities. (Crunden 1994)

As multiculturalism advances to the front and center of American lives, especially in academic centers, it is here that traditional mainstream

American society begins to feel uncomfortable, moody, and start to show their multicultural biases. Any indicator that multiculturalism reduces the prevailing and traditional monolithic/monotype dominating culture's well-being, is viewed as a threat to the psychological imbalance of mainstream Americans. (Spindler 1963) It is here where the author connects this subject of this work to multiculturalism. As an American society, we are bombarded daily with issues that affect us psychologically, physically, socially, and emotionally, just like any other society. Unlike most of those societies, America's ethnographies (cultural descriptions) are countless. Like most of those societies European culture dominate, especially in political power, running of the affairs of state, controllers of the purse strings, tax distributions, and distributors of the wealth. Not only is this true by present standards, but also by traditional standards. (Jorgenson, Truzzi 1974)

In America, this is no less true. The many problems associated with cultures, cultural diversity, multiculturalism, racism, cultural sensitivity, and political correctness, begs the following questions more than ever: Who are we as Americans? What are we doing as Americans? What should we be doing as Americans?

The fact is Americans are no different than any other people, societies, ethnicities, or cultures, in terms of our humanity. All human beings are subject or affected by the environment of which they are born into. (Jorgenson, Truzzi 1974)

The external force of other societies affects human beings in their natural environment whether their material, physical, political, social, ideological, or their economical system. These institutions, viz.(namely) family, governments, schools, churches, synagogues, mosque, temples, other places of religious worship, and health-care facilities, are all part of our cultural experience and development. Even our places of employment, banks, recreational and other social outlets, are all part of the psychological makeup, and therefore affect every American. Culture constructs itself no matter how poor or wealthy, educated or illiterate, the color-of-skin, race, language, ethnicity, or geographical location.

As human beings, we respond humanely to the environment we are a part of in order to extract from that environment the necessities for survival. All humans in societies respond physically, psychologically, economically, politically, socially, spiritually and emotionally to their environment. This is also true of Americans whether in our similarities or in our diversities. (Garretson 1976)

THEODUS JORDAN

Here lies the author's thesis: The increase in cultural influx of ethnicities, cultural diversity, multiculturalism, transnational America—a term Randolph Bourne (1997) has articulated as representative of all cultures. This term also represents the mass immigration that took place at the turn of this century, i.e., the twenty-first century. This increased attention in culture, cultural diversity, and multiculturalism in recent years has begun to change this society from a monolithic/monotype society, to a society which has begun to recognize that one culture does not fit all of a society's needs; whether such needs are in fact cultural, educational, philosophical, religious or spiritual, or most assuredly, psychological in nature. Nor is the application for addressing these varied human needs can be remedied by one cultural psychoanalytical model or psychotherapeutic intervention.

Most of the textbooks and mainstream language and data in today's mental health and academic curricula seem to confuse more than it clarifies. For example, most text seems to categorize diversity into three groups: ethnic, gender, and racial. Rarely, do they use the color-of-skin, language, or religion on the surface. As a result, there is the tendency to over generalize and stereotype people, which leave hidden the many significant and important contributions made by these groups to the whole and good of society's imagination. (Bourne 1997)

This overgeneralization of any group of people's importance further relegates them into lower levels of importance; thus, destroying them while robbing them of their essence and self-esteem; leaving them to dry out and die, or forever remain in a state of poverty and suspension forever, thereby allowing them to form into another type of cultural group that weighs even more heavily upon the economy than before. (Bourne 1997)

While it is for sure that the further splintering of these cultural groupings, spurned by over generalizing them from the start, contribute to more unchecked diversity. The external forces coupled with the internal forces of feelings of insignificance and so forth. Both create to generate new and different sets of issues that are detrimental to the whole of the society. This research suggests to this author that there are unavoidable pathological patterns that very visible in our present American system; and are therefore preventable, treatable, and containable. (Bourne 1997)

Danny Wedding, coauthor of his book, *Current Psychotherapies 7th Edition*, notes in his article "Contemporary Issues" (*American Psychological Association* 2002) that cultural diversity poses difficulties for therapist [who] remain uninformed about the cultural values of their clients, as well as therapist who respond to clients on the basis of cultural stereotypes.

He goes on to say, "striking the proper balance between cultural sensitivity and stereotyping requires clinical acumen and an understanding of and appreciation for cultural differences." Since Freud, we have moved through the centuries, especially in the eighteenth and nineteenth centuries, to a time when emotional disorders and disorganized thinking was mostly the responsibilities given to ministers, priest, or kept out of sight and in homes. Then mental illness was given to the physicians as psychiatry steadily developed into a discipline of its own right. (Beck 1990)

Like all societies, we are impacted by the rising number of immigrants that are coming to the shores of America, also by the changing of the guard and what has been constituted as the traditional approaches to psychotherapies. Multiculturalism, coming together in this great melting pot called America, interacts in a forever-changing economy, where racial differences, classes, religions, politics, the length of time in American society, one's cultural historical experiences, and the degrees of discrimination already experienced, forces inevitable changes. (Sue, Ivey, Pederson 1996)

Today, unfortunately, not all groups recognize and receive multiculturalism as a positive entity upon traditional America. There is a conservative backlash against multiculturalism, led by those with a very narrow view of what America can become.

In every aspect of American life, and no less true in all health fields, "the white therapist have a long way to go," says Monica McGoldrick, Joe Giordano, and John k. Pearce, in their classic work and textbook called *Ethnicity and Family Therapy, 2nd edition* (1996). Family therapy treats race and ethnicity as a special issue, not a basic factor. This is a problem for white ethnics in recognizing their true relationships to other cultural groups. As patriarchy, class hierarchies, heterosexist ideologies have been invisible structural definers of all European groups' ethnicity, so have race and racism been invisible definers of European groups' cultural values.

The therapist today has to learn to appreciate cultural variability, another way of saying, multiculturalism. Helping a client to resolve conflict and achieve a stronger sense of self may require the therapist to forego traditional roles in application of psychotherapeutic methods. It could very well require unlocking a family's cultural history held by years of family secrets and feuding embedded inside an ethnic tradition. A part of the process of getting through this kind of conflict may require the therapist to learn to identify and consciously be able to select the correct ethnic values needed in order to penetrate the client's taboo field.

The family may need coaching to get beyond its emotional negative field of allowing the therapist access to long-held family secret value zones. Such a therapist must have the type of gregarious attitude, which can only come from being both familiar and comfortable with cultural groups. (Baruth/ Manning 2003)

The Paradoxes and Contradictions of Multiculturalism:

As in all newly born phenomenons, there are paradoxes and contradictions. There are matters of new values verses old values being replaced by newer ideas. This is no less true when it comes to how "multiculturalism" plays out in the American arena as America began to focus and readjust its sails to deal in the new millennium on "multiculturalism" in the 21st. Century. Sometimes the conflict is within the concept itself. Such as the values that are inherently found within the concept of "multiculturalism". These new values, no matter how noble, superior, or inclusive, they present themselves, are still demanding, intrusive, even when these appear to be healthy to society. These values compete to live in an environment formerly dominated by traditional values it must now replace in most cases . . . values, which have been held by a majority in longevity. It does not matter how well intentioned the new values are—even if one believes in such new values as being better for them . . . One still has to overcome the sense of loss, displacement, and the replacement of long-held established mores. However, this author believes that such actions are still necessary in order that "multiculturalism" thrives.

The problem of the ideal and all inclusive multicultural expression, inevitably, comes into conflict with settled cultural expression and its long-held monopoly upon culture and values of its own. The real conflict here is not so much as replacing values but as expanding values to become inclusive in a democracy whose goals are true equality, justice, and liberty for all. Especially, when wealth is to be equally distributed based on mass-collected generated tax revenues.

Another contradiction or constant conflict is in the way the American culture responds to its own belief system. Most Americans believe in equality but recognize equality only by class and not with the mobility to access opportunity, particularly, if you are viewed from the outset as poor. Though in our hearts, "equal opportunities" suggest that everyone has the same opportunity to pursue goals and achieve the American dream, yet the existence of poverty, racism, prejudice, and discrimination are inherent contradictions . . . even as the American culture emphasizes "individualism" and "equality" simultaneously. This precludes many from full-participation into this "Democracy". Many people, because of this, are labeled and therefore become stymied.

Summary:

Finally, multiculturalism has become a national identity. It explores the changing American thinking. It seizes upon the long-held concepts of what an American democracy is all about. It questions the very sanctity and sanity of this ages' beliefs and values. It digs into the "psyche" of those gone on before to challenge those who remain here-and-now, with terms like equality, truth, honesty, fairness, liberty, and justice for all, and what these terms meant in the minds of those fore-writers and the signers of an American Constitution? (Beck 1990)

While it is inconceivable that they could not see beyond legalized slavery, some must have had fleeting thoughts. Perhaps they could not see beyond their *superiority complexes,* for it appears that multiculturalism has evolved in spite of their lack of multicultural vision. Now, in the present milieu, adjustments have to be made. This author and others like him are turning to counseling psychology to help us navigate our way through this mind-field of the psychological babble. Hopefully, we will help others in the process find literacy, then voice.

CHAPTER 3

The Relevance of Existentialism to "Counseling Psychology"

Definition: Existentialism—A philosophy that emphasizes the uniqueness and isolation of the individual experience in a hostile or indifferent universe. (the American Heritage Dictionary;2nd. Col.Edt.;1991.)

EXISTENTIALISM, as this author has attempted to define it in the introduction of this work, has two schools of thought experienced by Western thinkers. Those who have been in the vanguard of shaping the American psyche from the beginning of the brutal European explorers, to the slaughter of the Native American, the enslavement and colonization of the African American, the forced segregation of the races, the imperialism of European rule, and quest for the "Manifest Destiny" of the American white man. (Nevins, Commager 1962)

However shocking as this may seem, this is not the only picture of America which this author sees. There is and must be another view which has led to one of the greater nations on earth. This is why this author feels it is important to explain, in some depth, the school of thought, which has guided the American psyche from its inception. There is also another reason. The foundation this author is attempting to lay in order for the reader to begin to understand the title of this work. The reader could not have the full benefit or the basic conceptualization of how this author is attempting to present, how counseling psychology is in need of revamping its psychotherapeutic applications in order to accommodate a multicultural audience in this 21st century. (James 1990)

The existentialism reported on in this work is not about a state of becoming or about the "becoming being," but a state of being. "The faculty of being is Imagination," says Rollo May, existentialist and psychologist, in his work with H. Ellenberger in 1958, *Existence: a New Dimension in Psychiatry and Psychology*.

Much earlier on, Friedrich Nietzsche, a German philosopher born in Rockne, Prussia in 1844, was a brilliant student at Leipzig who later became a professor of classical philology (specialized study of languages and literature) and Soren kierkegaard, a Danish philosopher and theologian, both became the leading influences in the existentialism movement. Both Nietzsche and Kierkegaard are regarded as the two representing views, or schools of thought, on existentialism. They were for two reasons.

One is, they had been taught and shaped largely by Europe and its traditional philosophical concepts, which included religion—the science of their day and world literature and its influences. Religious freedom was still a new and growing phenomenon. There were many sects and religions. In America, such religious concepts were being influenced greatly by the Judaea-Christian model practiced by the Catholic Church and through the Protestant Reformation Churches. (Reese 1980a)

Second, there were two reigning views of religion: the humanistic view and the Supernatural. Or, the atheistic existentialist view of (Nietzsche) and, the theistic existentialist view of (Kierkegaard) represent both the secular and spiritual sides of the psyche but not a Multicultural view of America. (Reese,1980)

To be sure, existentialism has its origin in the works of Nietzsche and "the God is dead" (atheistic) movement, declaring that each individual must seek his own values, providing a bridge to the future for himself. kierkegaard, on the other hand, felt also that the individual was subjective to himself and that angst or anguish was the central emotion to human life; but with respect to God, kierkegaard stressed the need for a "leap of faith." (Reese, 1980b)

All other philosophers of existentialism fall among these two basic thoughts of Nietzsche's atheism or Kierkegaard's theism. Existentialism started as a philosophical movement challenging essentialism. It appears that the argument centered on the questions of what constituted matter in contrast to form, or is *existence* in contrast to *essence*. The mind can more readily deal with essence and form because these are within the realms of comprehension and cognition. (Reese 1980c)

According to these philosophers of old—including Plato, q.v. 1; Aristotle, q.v.* 7; Thomas Aquinas, q.v. 5,6; Duns Scotus, q.v. 5; kant, q.v. 5; Hegel, q.v. 5,6: kierkegaard, q.v. 1,7: Brentano, q.v. 3; Husserl, q.v. 6; Russell, q.v.4; Heidegger, q.v. 1,4,5; Weiss, q.v.—existence is one of four modes of being, standing alongside actuality, ideality, and God. Sartre, q.v. 2; and Quine, q.v. 2, adds the following: *matter* and *existence* are more elusive, distant, and other than conscious. (*q.v. = quoted verse) (Aristotle 1939)

Thus, existence and matter are less grasping as substances with definition, shape, form, and discernable properties, which the human mind can readily bring into its focus of human understanding and measure. Therefore the movement is born and centered on the word *existence*, from the Latin *ex* and *sisters*, meaning to "step forth or emerge." Obviously the word takes on its noun form of *existentialism*, as it means existence. As it became a philosophical movement, it became known as existentialism. (Reese 1980)

As with any new philosophical concept, there were two schools of thought, the secular view of existence and the religious view of our existence: Did humans evolve or were they created? Did we produce ourselves, or, was there an outside force or designer? Who gave to us form, shape, and being? As this author has stated above and in the introduction of this work, the two schools of thought were led by Nietzsche (atheistic—man is self-existing), and kierkegaard (theistic—God is man's leap of faith). (Reese 1980)

So then, the less-than-obvious questions to be asked during these earlier days that divided the theist and the atheist are as follows: The question of essence; does a person, thing, idea, or entity, have essence? Where does it get its form? Its shape? Its definition? And wherefrom can be explained; and whereto does it go? How do we exist, or does existence as an entity give birth to essence? The former forms the basis of the theist. The theist or essence formed being. A being forms existence, and not the other way around. The atheist puts forth: your existence determines your essence and your being; without essence first, you have no existence or reason for being. (Reese 1980)

Relevance to Theme:

What is the relevance and connection of the above with the subject matter? The history and influence of Western thought based upon the American psyche is the short answer. All history in America is connected to this thinking . . . i.e. "how America has been cultivated, socialized, and cultured by the philosophical "masters" of its past?" The point here of course is for this author to demonstrate how this philosophy is related to the present, here-and-now, subject matter? To examine: what is existentialism? How existentialism is impacted by the influx of multiculturalism since these great thinkers? (All of whom, by the way, were white, male, European, in their thinking. This is not said to minimize their impact and great contributions to shaping of American values and beliefs . . . to in the least) (Hirschfield 1968)

The author now feels that the reader understands the concept of existentialism, and how and why, it is necessary for the understanding of how existentialism is essential in changing the way counseling psychology must be applied to a new and different generation made up a multiculturals— each vying for equal recognition. And this is only the beginning of the twenty-first century. This brings us back to the modern-day trends in American existential psychotherapy led by such scholars and giants in the field as Rollo May, PhD, and Irvin D. Yalom, MD

A practicing psychiatrist at Stanford University, Palo Alto, California and Yalom had written the first book on a definition for existential psychotherapy. He entitled it, *Existential Psychotherapy*. But it was Rollo May, H. Ellenberger, and E. Angel who published their first major work in 1958, entitled *Existence: a New Dimension in Psychiatry and Psychology* (Yalom 1981; May 1961).

Paradoxes:

These scholars and practitioners were the vanguards of American-applied psychotherapeutic application. They were also first in attempting to pull away from the strict psychosexual Freudian influence which had dominated psychoanalysis thinking throughout the nineteenth century. These new and bold thinkers ushered in a new approach called existential psychoanalysis where psychoanalysis rested on the existentialist rather than

Freudian thought. Psychoanalysis for the existentialist psychotherapist as stated in chapter one, was different and living in an age of transition (Freud 1914). While the existentialists were looking for ways to understand human beings in a more reliable hands-on approach manner, during the early 40s and 50s, they were also concerned whether the patients being seen were really getting their issues and needs met. The existentialist therapists were the first to begin broadly defining existential therapy. (May 1961)

According to the existentialist, psychotherapeutic counselors believe that the individual human being possesses the ability to transcend time and space. This capacity to transcend is connected to our "ontological" nature (knowledge of being), an acute awareness, of self, being, and existence. (kean 1982, 2001)

Summary:

And finally, the existentialist therapist is "concerned with rediscovering the living person amid the dehumanization of our modern day culture" because existentialism allows for the consideration of such social factors as being, meaning, existence, essence, freedom choice, and anxiety, then the purpose of this work has been relevant to the subject matter in this multicultural environment. Looking again at psychotherapy gives the existentialist therapists his tools, his gifts. All human experience is part of a larger human condition. Existentialism is predicated and rooted in this philosophical history. This is precisely how, and why, multiculturalism impacts existentialism.

CHAPTER 4

Combining the Three Issues into a Single Theme

(i.e. Counseling Psychology/Multiculturalism/Existentialism)

Relevance:

THE DRIVING THEME for bringing these three modalities into an integrated discussion for this subject matter has been the results of changing trends in current psychotherapies reprinted as presented in the Weddings/Corsini book, *Current Psychotherapies, 7th Edition* (2005).

The entire text outlines the psychotherapies as reviewed in psychotherapy as shown in the introduction seem to be promoting a somewhat American renaissance and how psychotherapy has been changing in American culture since the 1900s, amid many views on Freud, also how American psychologist, therapist, and counselors have been developing their own variations, theories, and newer applications, methods, trends, and approaches to psychotherapy.

Admittedly, Danny Wedding and others, like Irvin Yalom, acknowledge in both their books, respectively, that cultural diversity and multiculturalism and the values and cultural differences are weighing in heavily as these impact how psychotherapy is applied in today's society. Also, it is slowly being recognized that the field of psychotherapy has been slack in preparing for the influx that multiculturalism is ushering into the American psyche. How the concept of counseling is changing dramatically as it responds to the social, political, economic forces which are shaping the clinical practices, in this 21st century is why this author is inquiring into this subject matter? The point here is how all of these forces are affecting counseling psychology and psychotherapy at this time as clinicians apply traditional theories and methodologies to the forever changing multicultural environment in which we are living in today. This is what Irvin Yalom, has called the here-and-now.

The here-and-now must indeed be applied to the clinical situation involving the interaction of client and clinician (Yalom 2002).

In another of his many books, *The Theory and Practice of Group Psychotherapy, 4th Edition* (2005), Irvin Yalom lends his expert knowledge to this author's hypothesis without realizing it. He explains that, "therapy, indeed, helps clients." He further says in chapter one of this textbook, that there are "therapeutic factors." These factors "govern the natural lines drawn dividing and distinguishing the therapeutic experience, altogether." He says there are **eleven** of these primary factors: [Paraphrases and Quotes are used here in relating these *primary factors*]

The Instillation of hope—a client in therapy long enough so that therapeutic factors can take effect on the client *in* the group, then, the group as well . . . These sets up *Universality:* Universality is the tendency for the client in a clinic or group session to think that he/she is uniquely themselves in connection to their thoughts, impulses, fantasies, or unacceptable problem. The earlier the clinician can dispel client's feelings of uniqueness, the quicker the client can begin to feel power and a sense of relief.

"There is no human deed or thought that lies fully outside the experience of other people," says Yalom (2005). Under this universality factor, Yalom (2005) inserts a very pertinent statement here: "The universality factor, like all the other of Yalom's therapeutic factors, universality does not have sharp borders, it merges with other therapeutic factors." His point here is, as clients perceive others and share their deepest concerns; all the clients will benefit and are more willing to share their stories.

Thus, their intimate lives with each other which often are where the healing process begins. The same is happening in the one-on-one with the clinician. The clinician is seeking the here-and-now conscious level with the client so that the client can feel more and more comfortable during the session. Thus, when more relaxed, a patient feels more familiar and more secure. The client then is supposedly less inhibited to share feelings, revealing more and more about self . . . (Yalom 2005)

Thusly, releasing pent-up emotional anxieties held inside for years because of the feelings of uniqueness in this way. Also Yalom's (2005) universality factor makes his only reference this author has noted, in all of Yalom's writings to multiculturalism. He points out, "In multicultural groups, the therapist may need to pay attention to the clinical factor of universality. Cultural minorities in a predominantly Caucasian group may feel excluded because of their different cultural attitudes toward disclosure, interaction, and affective expression. The Therapists must help the group move past a focus on concrete cultural differences to Transcultural—that is, Universal—responses to human situations and tragedies."

At the same time, Yalom (2005) goes on to say, the therapist must be keenly aware of the cultural factors at play. Mental health professionals are often sorely lacking in knowledge of the cultural facts of life required to work effectively with culturally diverse members. It is imperative that therapists learn as much as possible about their clients' cultures as well as their attachment to or alienation from their culture. Yalom makes this author's point of why this subject matter has validity, given his years of profound and distinguished scholarship, and well established credentials.

Imparting information:
It indicates information given by the expert in this field about mental illnesses, mental health, and general psychodynamics given by the therapist.

Didactic Instruction:
It means formal instruction; moral functioning, the meaning of symptoms, interpersonal and group dynamics, and the process of psychotherapy.

Altruism:
Altruism means learning how to feed others by extending an extra hand. (Yalom 2005) The corrective recapitulation of {a given} primary family group—is the idea of setting up the therapy sessions in a way that resembles the maladaptive primary family group.

The Development of Socializing Techniques:
It means the development of basic social skills. This, according to Yalom (2005), is a therapeutic factor that operates in all therapy groups. However, the nature of the skills taught and the explicitness of the process vary greatly, depending on the type of group therapy.

Imitative Behavior:
This means the modeling behavior of the therapist during a psychotherapeutic session by sitting, walking, talking, as well as thinking like him.

Interpersonal learning:
It is a broad complex therapeutic factor. Three concepts in understanding this particular factor, they are: the importance of interpersonal relationships; the corrective emotional experience; and the group as social microcosm. Understanding these three concepts shows how the psychotherapist can choose the right combination to insure interpersonal learning is taking place within each session.

Group cohesiveness
Cohesiveness is the group-therapy analogue to relationships in individual therapy. This therapeutic factor is essential to group participation regardless of the physical, mental, or social makeup of any group. (Yalom 2005)

Catharsis
Catharsis is interwoven with other therapeutic factors and therefore the least of all factors that will stand alone. (Yalom 2005)

Existential factors
All therapeutic factors existentialism (being, existence, morality, responsibility, freedom, the harsh realities of life and living, constructing our own life design) as searching for meaning even though thrown into a world that has no intrinsic meaning, according to Yalom. Both therapist and client come to recognize the following as basic signs that they both have come into the here-and-now: Recognize that life is unfair; that ultimately, you cannot avoid or escape some pain, struggle, and death. **you must recognize that no matter how close you get or come to depend or rely on others—no matter who they are—you still must learn to face life alone.** (Yalom 1981) **one must face basic issues of life and death, and then start to live life more honestly and less caught up in trivialities. and finally, you must take full responsibility for your life no matter how much guidance, teachings, or support you get from others. (yalom 2005)**

In a society as complex and diversified as America with a constantly growing multicultural influx, it is encumbered upon the nation of America to come to grips with what it is facing, that is, the shift in cultural thinking. (Sartre 1968) The monotype/monolithic and European cultural model mentioned in chapter two have been the American model since America began. The treatment of those who are maladaptive within this monotypic experience has also been singularly directive based in this monotypic approach and practice of treatment for all the psychological problems developed throughout the history of America's mental framework and structure. (Yalom 1981). In a forever-growing and diversified American culture, neither the family, nor the extended family, the religious institutions, our educational systems, not even our health institutions, will be able to keep pace with the rate of the growing psychological problems brought by the influx of multiculturalism. (Baruth 2003)

This author contends that this statement above only exposes one side. Only the external view and size of the American dilemma as it begins to look at her. Begin to test its cultural experience in American history, its values, principles, beliefs, ideals in a larger context—even globally. (*American Psychological Association*, 2002)

There remains, however, the other side of the coin, buried deeply and intrinsically but not hidden anymore—*Racism*! Will its dominance and stronghold over American culture ever relinquish in order for Americans to truly achieve true democracy? That is, equality, justice, fairness, equal distribution of revenues and social security, comparable wages and capital job ownership, equal access to credit, equal access to home ownership, and mortgages, and lastly, but most important, access to healthcare and prescription drugs. (Livermore 1968)

The organizational structures of the American system, that is, its educational, political, economical, governmental, as well as its religious institutions are all considered systems of acculturations. That is, they acquire, cultivate, and transmit culture. Since, as this author has so shown in chapter two of this work, culture is learned, not inherited. Amply, being born into America, or any country, does not give you culture, it only gives citizenship. (Norcross 1992) Cultivation is the psychosocial acculturation whereby all human beings breeds acquire culture. Multiculturalism expands, decentralizes, and diversifies and calls into question why anyone's culture should dominate in any multicultural settings. (Ramirez 1991)

This author believes that the more balance and significance assigned to multiculturalism and the respect of its influx into an American milieu, the less and less America will experience maladaptive social and psychological disorders coming from our general population. Is this an over-simplification? No, not at all, when you think about how the world is functioning by today's standards in the context of its traditional European construct. (Rosenblatt 1992)

The effectiveness of psychotherapy, as related to this author, during this course of study in counseling psychology, none have been more illuminating and transparent than the work in learning about the various psychotherapeutic approaches presented in the person-centered class; and the individual psychotherapy of Rogerian example.

This "Group Dynamics and Couples" courses on psychotherapy have been invaluable in helping this author formulate his theories concerning the direction and themes of where counseling psychology should and will be taking this field of study in the twenty-first century. In the Human Development course, it isolates the individualistic aspect of human development.

These courses have guided this author in making his decision to write on this subject for this IRP. The knowledge gained in each of those courses gave this author the insights and confidence needed in order to establish the basic concepts which has guided the gathering of research employed in the development of his theories leading to this theme.

Summary:

Finally the theories of development as understood from the Human Development course, provided for this writer all the evidence needed for the development necessary in establishing the psychosocial and scientific background for the understanding of how counseling psychology is affected by multiculturalism and existentialism in the way psychotherapy is applied and approached in this 21st century. (Rosenblatt 1992)

In defining each of these entities by showing their historical and developmental properties then outlining the concepts that formulated these into existence, this author has created an identifiable discipline of inquiry which is why the task and purpose of this project was given impetus from its outset.

The works of Sigmund Freud, Erik Erikson, Jean Piaget, and Lawrence kohlberg helped this author to concretely seal why this subject is most important and relevant to the discussion of psychotherapy today. A brief history will help to explain.

Erikson was born in 1902 in Frankfurt, Germany. He grew up in a place called karlsruhe, probably a Jewish township in Frankfurt. The threat of fascism drove Erikson and his family to the United States in 1933.

The fact that he had no college degree did not keep him from obtaining a position at the Harvard Medical School as Boston's first child analyst. Erikson was constantly concerned with the rapid changes occurring in America shown in both his writings, *Childhood and Society* (1950) and *Identity: Youth and Crisis* (1968). Erikson's (1959) concern with issues of the generation gap, racial tensions, juvenile delinquency, changing sexual roles, and the nuclear arms race are relevant to this author.

The point and relevance here is how Erikson looked into the culture and saw it as the psychosocial development of how the personality is shaped by its environment in very much the same as the fetus is shaped by the nurturing of the womb inside its mother. "Like the fetus, the personality becomes increasingly differentiated and hierarchically organized as it unfolds in, and is shaped by, a particular environment. There is movement through a set of psychosocial 'crises or issues as the child matures, and there is an expansion of his radius of significant relations . . .'" (Erikson 1968)

Piaget (Jean) was born in 1986 in Neuchâtel, Switzerland. Like his father, Piaget developed an inquisitive and critical mind. He, like his father, was not afraid to pick a fight when he found some historical truth being twisted to "fit some respectable traditions." Piaget's relevance to this author can be summed up by his own lifelong fascination with the "how humans comprehend the world." The branch of philosophy which concerned him the most was the study of knowledge, called epistemology. For Piaget (1952), epistemology is "the problem of the relationship between the acting or thinking subject and the objects of his experience."

Piaget (1963) tackled the same questions which have plagued philosophers for centuries: How do we come to know something? Is objective knowledge, unbiased by the nature of the knower, even possible? Are there certain innate ideals, or must all knowledge be acquired? Throughout his work and lifetime, Piaget seemed to be answering these questions in different content areas such as mathematics, moral reasoning, and language. Piaget was led to and through many different schools—philosophy, biology, history, mathematics, and psychology before coming to developmental psychology.

He concluded, but revolutionized thinking of how we as humans come to knowledge (epistemology)—knowledge as a process rather than as a state. It is an event or a relationship between the active knower and the known—a child knows or understands a ball or rattles by acting on it—physically or mentally. In a sense, people "construct" knowledge. They have active part in the process of knowing and even contribute to the form that knowledge takes. (Piaget 1952)

Cognitive humans actively select and interpret information in the environment. They do not passively soak up information to build a storehouse of knowledge. Children's knowledge of the world changes as their cognitive system develops. As the knower changes, so does the known . . . there is a constant interaction between the knower and the external world." (Piaget 1963)

Lawrence kohlberg, another of the developmental psychologist, is relevant to this discussion because he inserts the stage theory of the development of moral reasoning into scientific method. kohlberg (1958) postulates: most developmental theorists see morality as a basic dimension of a person's adaptation to his/her work. Although different theorists define moral behavior and development in markedly distinct ways, all ideas about moral functioning suggest an adjustment by the person to the social world, an adjustment that serves the dual purpose of fitting the person to his or her society, and at the same time, contributing to the maintenance and perpetuation of such a society. Thus moral development appears to be a basic component of human adaptation and societal survival. (kohlberg 1963a; 1963b)

Sigmund Freud, as stated in the introduction of this work is the premier foundation to all psychoanalytical theory both in an historical context and methodological context. Without his pioneering work into psychoanalytical theory and the vital force of knowledge and insight which has emerged and even expanded because of it, neither developmental psychology nor our understanding of the psychosocial world around us would still be lagging and holding. (Freud 1940; 1964)

Anne Anastasi, a developmental psychologist wrote in her now-famous article in the *Psychological Review* in 1958, on the Nature-Nurture controversy ("Does heredity or environment—nature or nurture determine the source of behavior?)

> Those who posed the issue in this way were assuming the reality of only one source of behavior; that is, in splitting the world into the real and the pseudo-phenomenal, the assumption was made that the independent, isolated action of one or the other domain provided a source of a behavior. However, we should reject this split way of posing the problem, because it is illogical.

Nature is heredity, and nurture is environment. The "which one" question assumes that heredity and environment are independent, separable sources of influence, and as such, that one can exert an influence in isolation from the other. If this was true, there would be no one in an environment without heredity, and there would be no place to see the effects of heredity without environment. Genes do not exist in a vacuum, says Anastasi. They exert their influence on behavior in an environment. At the same time, if there were no genes (and consequently no heredity), the environment would not have an organism in it to influence. Accordingly, nature and nurture are tied together. In life, they never exist independent of the other. Nature and nurture are always completely involved in all behavior. Put another way,

100% of nature and 100% of nurture always make their contributions to all behavior. Any method of inquiry into the source of behavioral development that does not take cognizance of this statement, seeks to make only artificial distinctions between nature and nurture which can lead only to conceptual confusion and an empirical blind alley. (Anastasi 1958)

In essence, by combining the views of each of these scientists, whose scientific approach is vastly different from the other and widely apart, all seem to come together on the one part that makes this author's work both vital and relevant to counseling psychology, i.e. it is a formal scientific theoretical construct with a set of functional interconnected, interrelated, ideals, axioms, postulates, hypotheses, variables, and laws congregated with an ethical inquiry and a beneficial one as well as an essential and vital entity needed if the goal of all people of goodwill is freedom, justice, equality, and fairness in this multicultural setting, called America.

METHODOLOGY

THERE WERE SEVERAL research methods (including computerized) used in this author's approach to this theme: a theoretical, a philosophical, an historical, a typological or comparative approach, a statistical, analytical, dialectical or augmentative, as well as a review of each course and discipline (includes all workshops) taken by this writer at the Cambridge College campuses.

Here, the writer found a wealthy and bountiful supply of books, articles, video/audio, as well as microfilm materials to help check and date facts which were out—dated, or facts which were unusual. The author's practical approach and experience as an educator was also drawn in compiling this work.

The Gutman Library of the Harvard Graduate School of Education in Harvard Square proved to be a convenient and wealthy source of material on the subject of education, culture, and diversity, also in cognitive and learning theory in human development. For example, in the Cambridge College Academic Catalogue 2004-2005, the definition this author needed which fitted the path of this work came through a course under Psychology, called Systems Thinking (PSY110). In order to get a fuller description of this course the author had to go on-line and use his password, student identification then enter the body of wealth of library materials at the Cambridge College Library system which includes the Gutman library connections.

Making use of the Cambridge College Online research links proved an invaluable resource: http://www.cambridgecollege.edu/student/research. cfm/. Cambridge College has provided this author with an extensive online resource for his academic research and personal education.

Not only did this resource method help this author in defining his subject, it also connected this author to how his subject is related to the understanding of himself in relationship to the larger world of counseling in psychology as related to every aspect of our world in general. For example, in the body of the text, the reader should notice immediately the definition, the meaning, and the operational terminology used. The reader should notice also how this research is used by this author in explaining the author's unapologetic claim to his theme. He declares it a theme worthy of consideration by the world of academia. Why? Because the research puts forth, in both philosophical and in scientific terms, a scientific method, for scientific discovery. The undisputed facts of history presented throughout this work and supported by the evidence revealed by this author's research, labeling, and chronicles of facts, are undeniable, statistically, methodically, and most surely, experientially. (See more statistics in section on limitations and the appendix sections of this work.)

The philosophical approach using the Socratic method of logic (as used by educators and western thought from the start of the American Dream phenomenon period until now) was used, whereby you start with a premise—as the subject of this work, so states a premises—then you move to the opposite of the stated premises which forces a conclusion. Hegel used this method with political and economic systems.

In his dialectical approach, Hegel used the terms *thesis* for premise, *antithesis* for diametrical view, and *synthesis* for the conclusion. Hegel (Georg Wilhelm Friedrich; 1770-1831) used these terms in explaining political and economical trends. But the point of the matter here is this author's approach to this subject matter should not be ignored of simple discarded as a discipline of study without further inquiry and critical evaluation. Disagreement with this subject matter should not be grounds for dismissal of it. This work, like all other academic work in any educational institution, should not be judged simply upon its content but rather upon the quality of its scholarship only.

Although the author named several methods used in the examination of this subject matter, it all boils down to basic research. Other research sources have been the Boston Public Library, which has volumes upon volumes of books, categories, and voluminous materials that proved to be immeasurable in its contribution to answering the author's most poignant questions on this subject. On multiculturalism (though there is very little done of the author's particular subject matter) there are unlimited volumes. On existentialism, there is no end to this subject matter (although some not necessarily connected to the author's work). The author had to find his own connectors.

ERIC, the Educational Resources Information Center provided by the United States government was essential as well as the American Counseling Association, Code of Ethics and many other state agencies too numerous to mention here. These were especially useful in helping to define counseling psychology as it is used today in therapeutic terms.

LIMITATIONS

T O THE SCHOLAR reading this work, it is obvious, that there are many limitations to this work. It does not have specific survey data. It simply puts forth a theory based on one's observation, experience, and empirical evidence. The evidence reflects both in research and experience. Plus, evidence from an historical and contemporary viewpoint . . . . Such evidence gathered through academic investigation as well as the social and scientific methods described to some extent, in the methodology section.

The definitions used in the discovery of this subject matter are operational. This means these definitions are functional and describes what the author is attempting to convey theoretically. These concepts, which are already known to an informed academic audience, are now being used philosophically, in terms of terminology, to extract, and construct a new course of study.

Hopefully, this author has succeeded in this accomplishment, or at least given pause for consideration that this subject is worthy of notation and thought in today's multicultural environment. The author has included all people-of-color, no matter what their individual ethnicity. Also, all white people have been cast in another category, breaking America down into two groups instead of the many other categories. Multiculturalism is defined not only by race, that is skin color, but also by language, custom, religion, cultural background, dress, creed, belief, and sexual orientation.

The idea here is to mesh all groups and cultures in a harmonious and coordinated melting pot where we all share equally in a common democracy. Diversity helps to keep our individualities, maintain our cultural identities, respect each other's values, and still share in a common democracy. Another limitation here may be for the reader who has extensive background in one of the areas defined in this study.

The author has postulated that counseling psychology is impacted by multiculturalism and existentialism. In defining these concepts, this author has gone to great length to present the history of these terms so that the reader is now open to less of an unfamiliar territory. He/she (the reader) should be able to grasp the precise meaning and gist of this author's thesis and connect the dots. There is no hidden agenda. The author's real hope is that this work lays the foundation for a series of works concerning racism within the historical context of American culture as seen from *inside* America by this author and others—blacks and whites.

Plainly speaking, in this twenty-first century and beyond, the author wishes to present *slavery* in terms never before presented, i.e., as a traumatic experience to be examined by scientific discourse as a discipline. in order to do this an understanding of the psyche (mindset) or the "thinking patterns" of americans in their cultural, developmental, historical, philosophical, social, economical, psychological, interpersonal, ecological, and political "conditioning," must be explained and put in perspective as it relates to *race*, here in america, both from america's inception (1492) and the signing of the "declaration of independence" (1776) and ingesting itself with a government "of," "for" and "by" the people and labeling itself a *Democracy*.

CONCLUSION

I F THE PURPOSE of this work has been to recognize that counseling psychology impacts both multiculturalism and existentialism, then the goal has been reached. In the introduction, this author has proclaimed that counseling psychology is driven by existentialism, while multiculturalism establishes itself by it . . . . Counseling psychology, as most psychotherapy and psychoanalysis, has its origin in European psychoanalytical theory, philosophy, and scientific methods:

Accordingly, not since Charles Robert Darwin (1809-1882) and his *Theory of Evolution* and the *Origin of the Species* with Alfred Russel Wallace, and their independent notions of natural selection, no scientist has impacted the world of psychiatry more than Sigmund Freud, who also founded psychoanalysis. An MD, Freud earlier in his career had collaborated with another well-known psychiatrist named Josef Breuer and the use of *hypnosis* in the treatment of hysteria of patients. From here, Freud began to develop his theories concerning free association as he began to reject *hypnosis* which "allowed material repressed in the unconscious to emerge to conscious recognition."

Freud was convinced that this undercharged emotional energy was sexual in nature. He and Breuer parted, leaving Freud to his own theories. In 1906, Freud was joined by Carl G. Jung and Alfred Adler. They, both psychiatrists, too parted with him also in protest over his emphasis on infantile sexuality and his theory of the Oedipus complex.

The point of the above short background of Freud is compelling indeed. His impact upon the world is just as profound and imbedded. Even though these scientist moved on to their respective fields of discovery, the basic structure of their analysis remain Freudian. The author's point is that this is also true of contemporary and popular psychology. Psychoanalysis, while it has undergone tremendous changes and structuring in its many differen forms, all such psychoanalysis, has had its origin-of-influence through the foundational works of Freud. That influence is the thread by which this author strings together his thematic claim, and, is why counseling psychology has to re-tool its psychological approach to how it conducts counseling in today's multicultural milieu.

Why? During Freud's time, before Freud and since Freud (1856-1939), Darwinism flourished (man came from the ape—and black people were considered 2/5 or 3/5 of a man by any white man's standards. This thought lasted until the new era of the civil rights movement led by Dr. Martin Luther king). The influence of Darwinism had its impact on the thinking of Freud and others during this time. Freud and others like him never expressed any animosity toward blacks as far as this author can read. But, the influence and the absence of mentioning of the earlier effects of slavery, segregation, and racism (Jim Crowism) in the apparatus of psychoanalytical theories compels this author to call into question whether one who counsels another without examining the entire historical affects of one's social and pathological experiences, has fully understood and embraced psychoanalysis in any form. Not to do so, must disqualify one as a fully authenticated counselor, as far as this author is concerned.

Surely as America becomes more and more *multicultural,* it has to rethink its European *mono*—cultural model, with its traditional influences, and consider what advantages the multicultural models presents and what it needs in order to replace the European mono-model. Counseling psychology as a discipline cannot rest or relax under its banner of "Manifest Destiny" (the concept and spread of a white man's prowess as conquerors of the world into a "one-nation" of superpower). The language of our society must become relevant to the existentialism of the masses which this author is presenting through this new phenomenon called *multiculturalism.*

PERSONAL STATEMENT

THIS AUTHOR MAKES no excuse for the completion of this work. The task has been daunting at best and totally not without its moments of complete physical and mental setbacks at worst. An eye and broken-face injury; and a hand-wrenching injury, both unprovoked hate-crimes by white assailants (Because this was a "White"-on-" Black crime, these assailants were never prosecuted or brought to justice, though they were known to the police and the courts). None of which kept me from completing all my full-time credits. This is the final project, though I almost did not make it. This IRP (Individual Research Project) for some reason proved to be more difficult than this writer had anticipated. Besides the procrastination, laziness, and just plain old reluctance to get it done, organizing the material was painstakingly excruciating. It was not just about writing another paper, though the writing was slow, it turns out that what this writer chose to write about was very basic to his beliefs, deeply imbedded and hidden in his soul.

It's as if this writer was both living and reliving his life simultaneously—two lives, one body. It seems that life's struggle became synonymous with writing the IRP. It was a day-to-day drudgery. The writer's own past, present (here-and-now) and future belief system had somehow come together, as if he was living all three lives at the same time and in the same space. The weights of life seemed heavier than at any other moment remembered, or experienced. The writer's mind seemed to have been totally consumed (completely occupied) with trying to figure out where he had been and where he wanted to go from here. This author did learn something in writing this essay with all its set-backs . . . that to live in the past is to live with "regret"; to live in the future is to live with "anxiety." Yalom says, and this author believes, that *reality* lives in the here-and-now. *Deal* in the present. Facing *reality* is a sign of *maturity* and *saneness*.

Every course of discipline this author has taken during his matriculation at Cambridge College has contributed to the writing of this work. It has also contributed to this author's regaining insight into himself, reconnecting with his past, and bringing it to the present where it can't seem so far away that it is never to be dealt with or neutralized.

This author believes in the relevance of this project and the future of counseling psychology as it relates to how we counsel or prepare to counsel America's new and different multicultural existentialist. As a teacher, minister, educator, and hopeful counselor, this author yearns for his day to show the world that multiculturalism can work as it brings out the best in all of us.

AUTHOR'S & READERS NOTE PAGE, 1

AUTHOR'S & READERS, NOTE PAGE,

REFERENCES

Adler, Alfred. 1931, 1958. *What life should mean to you*. New York: Capricorn Books.

—. 1969. *The science of living*. New York: Doubleday Anchor Books. American Psychological Association. 2002. *Ethical principles of psychologists and code of conduct*. Washington, DC: Author.

Anastasi, Anne. 1982. *Nature-nurture controversy: Psychological review And Testing*, 5th edition. New York: Macmillan

Arendt, Hannah. 1958. *The human condition*. Chicago: University of Chicago Press.

Aristotle. 1939. *Nichomachean ethics*, trans. H. Rackham Cambridge: Harvard University Press

Arlow, J.A. 1989. *Psychoanalysis and the search for morality*. In H. Blum, E.M. Winchell, and F. Rodman (eds). *The psychoanalytic core: Essay In honor of Leo Rangel* (pp.147-166) Madison, CT: International Universities Press.

Arlow, J.A. and Brenner, C. 1988. The future of psychoanalysis. *Psychoanalytic Quarterly*. Madison, CT: International University Press.

Aronson, Elliot. 1965. *The social animal*, 3rd Edition. San Francisco: W.H. Freeman and Company.

Bandura, Albert. 1969. *Principles of behavior modification*. New York: Holt, Rhinehart and Winston.

Baruth, L.C. and Manning, M.L. 2003. *Multicultural Counseling and Psychotherapy: A Lifespan Perspective*, 3rd Edition. Upper Saddle River: Prentice Hall.

Barrett, R.A. 1984. *Culture and conduct*, 2nd Edition. Belmont, CA: Wadsworth.

Beck, Aaron T., Freeman, A., and Davis, D.D. 2003. *Cognitive therapy and personality disorder*. New York: Plenum.

Beck, J.C. 1990. *Confidentiality versus the duty to protect: Foreseeable harm in the practice of psychiatry*. Washington, DC: American Psychiatric Press.

Bernstein, Richard J. 1978. *The restructuring of social and political theory*. Philadelphia: University of Pennsylvania Press.

Bion, J, ed. 1948. *Therapeutic social clubs*. London: Lewis

Bootzin, Richard R. & Bower, Gordon H., & Zajonc, Robert B., & Intro. By Asimov, Isaac. 1986. *Psychology today: An introduction* New York: Random House.

Bourne, Randolph S. 1997. *Randolph Bourne and the politics of cultural radicalism*. Lawrence: University of kansas Press.

Brunner, Borgna, ed. 2002. *Time Almanac: with information please*. Boston, MA: Family Education Company.

Corsini, Raymond J. 1956. *Freud, Rogers and Moreno. Group Psychotherapy*. Chicago, ILL: and-McNally.

—. 1968. Counseling and psychotherapy. In E.E. Borgotta and W.W. Lambert (eds.). *Handbook of personality theory and research*. Chicago: Rand McNally

—. 1991. *Five therapies and one client*. Itasca, Ill.: F.E. Peacock.

—, ed. 2001. *Handbook of innovative therapy*, 2nd Edition. New York: Wiley.

Corsini, Raymond J. and Rosenberg, B. 1955. Mechanisms of group psychotherapy. *Journal of Abnormal and Social Psychology*. Belmont, CA. {Start}

Corsini, Raymond J. and Wedding, D., ed. 2005. 5th Edition. Belmont, CA: Brook/Cole—Thomson Learning, Inc . . .

Crunden, R.M. 1994. *A brief history of American culture*. New York: Paragon House.

Dumont, F., and Corsini, R.J. 2000. *Six therapists and one client*. New York: Springer.

Ellenberger, H. 1970. *The discovery of the unconscious*. New York: Basic Books.

Ellis, Albert, and Dryden, W. 1997. *The practice of rational motive behavior therapy—REBT*. New York: Springer.

Ellis, Albert. 1962. *Reason and emotion in psychotherapy*. Secaucus, NJ: Citadel.

—. 1976. "The biological basis of human irrationality." *Journal of Individual Psychology*, pp. 145-168.

Erikson, Erik. 1950. *Childhood and society*. New York: Norton

—. 1968. *Young man Luther: A study in psychoanalysis and history*. New York: Norton

Frankl, Viktor E. 1975. *The unconscious God: psychotherapy and theology*. New York: Simon and Schuster.

—. 1959. *Man's search for meaning*. Boston: Beacon Press.

—. 1968. *Psychotherapy and existentialism: Selected paper on Logotherapy*. New York: Washington Square Press.

—. (1969, 1970). *The will to meaning: Foundation and Applications of logotherapy.* New York and Cleveland: The World Publishing Company. Also paperback, New York: New American Library

Freud, Anna. 1936. *The ego and the mechanisms of defense*: New York: International University Press.

—. 1951. Observations on child development. *Psychoanalytic study of Child,* 18-30.

Freud, Sigmund. 1901. *The psychopathology of everyday life.* (Standard Edition, Vol.6.).

—. 1911. *Formulations regarding the two principles of mental Functioning.* (Standard Edition, Vol6.).

—. 1914a *The history of the psychoanalytic movement* (Standard Edition; Vol. 14.).

—. 1905b.*Three essays on sexuality.* (Standard Edition, Vol. 7).

Feldman, F. 1968. : Results of psychoanalysis in clinic case assignments. *Journal of the American Psychoanalytic Association*, 274-300.

Fukuyama, M. 1990. *Taking a universal approach to multicultural counseling Counselor education and supervision.*

Gamst, F.C. and Norbeck, E. 1976. *Ideas of culture: sources and uses.* New York: Holt, Rinehart and Winston.

Garretson, L.R. 1976. *American culture: An anthropological perspective.* Dubuque, IA: Wm. C. Brown.

Gazda, G.M. 2001. *Life skills training.* In. R.J. Corsini (ed.) *Handbook of innovative therapy,* New York: Wiley.

Goldenberg, I., and Goldenberg, H. 2004. *Family therapy: An Overview,* 6th Edition. Pacific Grove, CA: Brooks/Cole.

Havilland, W.A. 1997. *Anthropolog y*, 8th Edition. Forth Worth, TX: Hartcourt Brace College Publishers.

Hirschfield, Charles, ed. 1968. *Classics of western thoughts: III. The modern world*. New York: Harcourt, Brace & World, Inc.

Horney, k. 1942. *Self-analysis*. New York: Norton.

James, William. 1955. *Humanism and truth, in pragmatism and four essay from the meaning of Truth*, EDT . . . Ralph Barton Perry. New York: Meridian Books.

Jung, C.G. 1935a, 1966. Principles of practical psychotherapy. *In the practice of Psychotherapy. Collected works*, Vol. 16, (pp. 3-20). Princeton: Princeton University Press.

Jorgenson, J.G. and Truzzi, M. (Ends). 1974. *Anthropology and American life*. Englewood Cliff, NJ: Prentice-Hall.

Jung, C.G. 1948, 1980. *Techniques of attitude change conducive to world peace in the symbolic life. Collected works*, Vol. 18 (pp. 606-613). Princeton: Princeton University Press.

Kean, Robert. 1982, 2001. *The evolving self*. Cambridge, Massachusetts: Harvard University Press.

Kierkegaard, Soren. 1954. *Fear, trembling, and the sickness until death*. Garden City, NY: Doubleday.

Kohlberg, Lawrence 1971. *Theory of moral reasoning development*. Stanford, CA: Stanford University Press

Kroeber, A. and kluckhohn, C. 1952. *Problems with culture: Definition*. New York: Holt, Rinehart, and Winston.

Lash, Christopher. 1965. *The new radicalism in America 1889-1963*. New York: W.W. Norton.

Lazarus, Arnold A. 1976. *Multimodal behavior therapy*. New York: Springer.

Levy, Judith S. and Greenhill, Agnes. 1983. *The concise Colombia Encyclopedia*. New York: Avon Books.

Livermore, J.M., Talmudist, C.P., and Meehl, P.E. 1968. *On the justification for civil commitment*, University of Pennsylvania: Law Review.

Mahrer, Alvin R. 1985. *Psychotherapeutic change: An alternative approach to Meaning and measurement*. New York: Norton.

May, Rollo. 1981. *Freedom and destiny*. New York: Norton.

—. 1961. *Existential psychology*. New York: Random House.

McGoldrick, Monica, Giordano, Joe, and Pearce, John k., eds. 1996. *Ethnicity & family therapy*, 2nd Edition. New York: The Guilford Press.

Moreno, Jacob L. 1946-1969. *Psychodrama* (vols; last two with Z. T. Moreno). Beacon, NY: Beacon House.

Naylor, L.L., ed. 1997. *Cultural diversity in the United States*. Westport, CT: Bergin & Garvey.

Nevins, Allen and Commager, Henry S. 1962. *A pocket history of the United States*. New York: Washington Square Press.

Nietzsche, Friedrich W. 1967, 1997. *The birth of tragedy and the case of Wagner*, ed. and trans. Walter kaufman. New York: Vintage Books. Lawrence: University of kansas Press.

Norcross, J.C., Alford, B.A., and DeMichele, J.T. 1992. The future of Psychotherapy. Delphi data and concluding observations. Psychotherapy: 150-158.

Painter, G. and Vernon, S. 1981. Primary relationship therapy. In R.J. Corsini (eds), *Handbook of innovative psychotherapies*. New York: Wiley.

Patterson, C.H. 1987. Comments. *Person-Centered Review*, 246-248.

Perls, Fredrick "Fritz." 1973, 1976. *The Gestalt approach and eyewitness to therapy*. New York: Bantam.

Piaget, Jean. 1976. *Needs and significance of cross-cultural research in genetic psychology*. B. Inhelder and H.H. Chipman (eds.), Piaget and his school. New York: Springer.

Piaget, J. 1978. *Success and understanding*. Cambridge, MA: Harvard University Press.

Puner, Helen Walker. 1961. *Freud: His life and his mind*. Foreword by Fromm, Erich. New York: Dell Publishing Company, Inc.

Ramirez, M. 1991. *Psychotherapy and counseling with minorities: a Cognitive approach* to individual and cultural differences. New York: Pergamum.

Reese, W.L. 1980. *Dictionary of philosophy and religion: eastern and western thought*. New Jersey: Humanities Press.

Reid, O.G., Mims, S., Higginbottom, L.,2005. Post Traumatic Slavery Disorder(PTSlaveryD) CONQUERING BOOkS, LLC.

Richardson, Jeanne E. 2005. *Introduction to Counseling*. Cambridge College: Counseling Psychology Department, Cambridge, Massachusetts.

Rogers, Carl R. 1986a. *Client-centered therapy*. In I.L. kutash and A. Wolf (eds). Psychotherapist casebook: *Therapy and technique in practice* San Francisco: Jossey-Bass

Rogers, Carl R. 1986b. *The dilemma of a South African white*. Person-Centered Review, 15-35.

Rosenblatt, A.D., Adler, G., Bemporad, J.R., Feigelson, E.B., Michels, R., Morrison, A. P., et.al. 1992. *Psychotherapy in the future*. Washington, DC: American Psychiatric Association.

Sartre, Jean-Paul. 1956. *Being and nothingness*. New York: Philosophical Library

—. 1968. *Existentialism.* New York: Vintage Books

Skinner, B.F. 1953. *Science and human behavior.* New York: Macmillan.

Spradley, J.P. and McCurdy, D. 1972. *The cultural experience.* Prospects Heights, IL: Waveland

Spindler, G., (1963). *Education and culture: Anthropological approaches*: New York: Holt, Rhinehart and Winston.

Spindler, G. and Spindler, L. 1993. *The American cultural dialogue and its Transmission.* Bristol, PA: Falmer Press.

Stewart, E.C. and Bennett, M.J. 1991. *American cultural patterns: A cross Cultural perspective* (revised edition) Yarmouth, MA: Intercultural Press.

Sue, D.W., Ivey, A., and Pederson, P. 1996. *A theory of multicultural Counseling and therapy* Pacific Grove, CA: Brooks/Cole.

Sue, D.W., and Sue, D. 2003. *Counseling the culturally diverse: Theory and Practice*, 4th Edition. New York: Wiley.

Sue, S., & Zane, N. 1987. *The role of culture and culture technique Psychotherapy American Psychologist.*

Vaillant, George E. 1993. *The Wisdom of the ego.* Cambridge, Massachusetts: Harvard University Press.

White, Morton. 1976. *Social thought in America: the revolt against formalism* London: Oxford University Press.

Wolpe, J. 1958. *Psychotherapy by reciprocal inhibition.* Stanford, CA: Stanford University Press.

Yalom, Irvin D. 1981. *Existential psychotherapy.* New York: Basic Books.

Yalom, Irvin D., and Leszcz, M. 2005. *The theory and practice of group psychotherapy*, 5th Edition. New York: Basic Books.

Yalom, Irvin D. 2002. *The gift of therapy*. New York: HarperCollins Publishers.

—. 1989. *Love's executioner*. New York: Basic Books.

LITERATURE IN REVIEW

U NDENIABLY, THE FOUNDATION for counseling psychology has been long laid and established for centuries now. The literature flourishes in the libraries, science books, hospitals, health facilities, and throughout our medical schools and their systems. In fact, the field of psychology is widening especially in the area of mental health and the need for both facilities and practitioners ready to step-up and become advocates for the many waiting clients.

There is increasing literature and innovative research on the mind/body connection. This research, unfortunately for this author, falls short when it comes to knowing how counseling psychology is jolted by multiculturalism in our everyday existential experience. In spite of this somewhat negligible void, there still seems to be a concordance between the individual personality dynamic and the psychotherapy innovation within the system progression and development. (Corsini 2005)

Accordingly, the world system of psychotherapy, which is imbedded in the counseling-psychological system started by Sigmund Freud in modern-day terms claims to be the very best definition for what therapy is and/ or what therapy represents, based on the works of Raymond J. Corsini, psychologist. (Corsini 2005)

The literature on defining psychotherapy, like counseling psychology, cannot be defined with any real precision. It could be defined as a formal process of interaction between two parties. Usually two parties, but there can also be other parties to join. Corsini goes on to say that, "if we were to examine various theories and procedures in psychotherapy we would find a bewildering set of ideas and behaviors."

The difficulty with defining both counseling and psychotherapy is because there are all kinds of therapies and all have a measure of counseling in them. What one authority considers psychotherapy maybe completely different from what another authority describes as therapy or counseling?

The literature, Corsini (1991) contends, suggests that counseling and psychotherapy are the same qualitatively; they differ only quantitatively. There is nothing that a psychotherapist does that a counselor does not do. Throughout this work, the author's wish is to define succinctly counseling psychology, but according to Corsini (2005), "no definition can be made that will include all counseling methods, all psychotherapies. He says there have been various attempts to separate the psychotherapies to exclude all counseling methods but these have failed."

The literatures also suggest that these terms, counseling and psychotherapy are interchangeable but have different meanings only to the various practitioners in the mental and medical healthcare various fields. According to the field of study in psychotherapy, the psychotherapist defines counseling as a relative short period. It occurs in one session and rarely goes more than five sessions. Psychotherapy, according to these practitioners, usually runs for many sessions and could last for years. (Horney 1942) Counseling is problem oriented, while psychotherapy is person oriented. (Patterson 1987)

The processes which occur in both counseling and psychotherapy are identical, say F. Dumont and R. J. Corsini (2000), but differ, relative to the time spent. As pointed out in the introduction and chapter one of this work, defining counseling psychology remains *elusive* but not without perimeters. It is the expertise, including experience, alertness, and maturity, and exposure of the counselor, the practitioners, and the psychiatrists who truly determine a definition for counseling or psychotherapy each time they meet with any particular client.

In further attempts to define counseling and psychotherapy, the literature suggests, by G.M. Gazda, *Life Skills* training taking from R.J. Corsini's *Handbook of Innovative Therapy* (Corsini 2001) in which counseling stresses the giving of information, advice, and orders by someone considered an expert in a particular area of human behavior. While psychotherapy is a process of helping people discover why they think, feel, and act in unsatisfactory ways. (Gazda 2001) A counselor is primarily a teacher, while a psychotherapist is a detective. (Painter and Vernon 1981)

In the chapter on multiculturalism, the literature is voluminous, but here again, none that speaks directly to this authors question of "how multiculturalism affects existentialism in the twenty-first century?" While this author's research centered on the term *multiculturalism*, most literature focuses on the term *culture* itself.

This author believes, based on the works of Anthropologist R.A. Barrett, that because of the traditional, historical, and literary approach to dealing with culture, it has been led by the field of Anthropology. The anthropologists have studied *cultures* individually and then formed universal patterns based on similarities and differences taken from within those individual systems of culture. (Barrett 1984)

Without the anthropologist today and surely of yesterday, scientific and other practitioners who seek to understand humans and their environment would be at a loss. Having acknowledged this truth, the author here feels, except for the word *culture* itself, the connection of how multiculturalism impacts existentialism in counseling psychology has yet to be made from the available literature.

However, the work of F.C. Gamst, and E. Norbeck, in their book entitled *Ideas of Culture: Sources and Uses* (1976), helps this author tremendously in this effort. These anthropologists have put together a collection of readings on culture in which the authors have examined the development of the "cultural concept" and all the ways it has been looked at and used. Their book became a basic reading for this author in trying to understand the cultural concept.

W.A. Havilland, in his book entitled, *Anthropology,* 8th edition (1997), helps this author further to understand the discipline of anthropology as it relates to the basic humans and the human experience. His book presents a straightforward and thorough knowledge of who, what, how, and substantive materials of the major subfields in *cultural* anthropology. The works of J.P. Spradley and D. McCurdy, called the *Cultural Experience* (1972), introduces to this author their ethnographic fieldwork. Their work examines the concept of culture in the complex setting of nation-states (*Nation-state* is a term used by anthropologist Larry L. Naylor to describe modern societies with clearly defined and recognized territorial boundaries that have reached the state level of political integration.). This work also produced the first ethnographies (cultural descriptions) of various groups in America (Naylor 1997).

G. Spindler and L. Spindler focused on *dialogue* that must be constant between competing interests in America. These authors provided an insightful discussion of the dominant values of the culture. They firmly believed that the basic elements of the American culture could be seen in the *dialogue.* Their book is entitled *The American Cultural Dialogue and Its Transmission.* (Spindler/Spindler 1993)

In *American Cultural Patterns: a Cross-Cultural Perspective* (1991) the authors, E.C. Stewart, and M.J. Bennett, take aim at intercultural relations. They seek to compare some cross-cultural patterns organized around the idea of cultural contacts, certain assumptions, perceptions, and values of Americans. Certain American traits are isolated out, analyzed, and compared with other cultures. This author sees this term being used for the first time as an exchange for multiculturalism. Also given this author the validity needed to use the term interchangeably with authenticity.

Existentialism, as used throughout this work, has many, many sources and volumes of materials because of the very nature and inherent essence of the word itself. It too, however, like the other terms used in this essay has not been challenged or called upon to produce any defense of how it affects multiculturalism or how multiculturalism affects it, in its impact upon counseling psychology? This author, in chapter three talks on existentialism and the basic two schools of thought influencing Europeans and Americans throughout the eighteenth, nineteenth, and twentieth centuries. Among these were the *Atheism* of Friedrich Nietzsche, the God-is-dead theme; and the *Theism* of Soren kierkegaard, the leap-of-faith doctrine. This author also mentioned the *earlier* influences of Charles Darwin (Darwinism) before these thinkers.

Later, there came the influences of Sigmund Freud (father of psychoanalysis) into the beginning of the twentieth century. In his book, *Denatured Nietzsche* (1997), Randolph S. Bourne offered ascendancy to the existence of assimilation to immigrants as an alternative to the Anglo-Saxon mold and its melting pot. He called it "Transnational America" versus the

Melting Pot. Instead, he used musical metaphors to describe how America should become an orchestra.

Finally, in Friedrich Nietzsche's work, The *Birth of Tragedy* (1997), he explores the inner history of self by tracing the birth of self-hood in our psychic life, and by exploring the price; we pay for its achievement.

APPENDIX

Statistics of an American Portrait

In creating a demographic portrait of Americans, the usual place to start is with the statistics provided by the United States Census. The United States Bureau of the Census based on the 2002 Almanac series; Times.

NUMBER   PERCENT

OVERALL WORLD POPULATION/INTERNATIONAL BY DECADES,

1950 .... 2050:
2,556,000,503 9,346,399,468

OVERALL U.S. POPULATION:

	NUMBER	PERCENT
Total Population—	281,421,906	100.0%
Male ^^	138,053,563	49.1%
Female ^^	143,368,343	50.9%

BY RACE:

	NUMBER	PERCENT
One Race (Non—Bi-racial)	274,595,678	97.6%
White	211,460,626	75.1%
Black or African American	34,658,190	12.3%
American Indian and Alaska Native	2,475,956	0.9%
Asian	10,242,998	3.6%
Asian Indian	1,678,765	0.6%
Chinese	2,432,585	0.9
Filipino	1,850,314	0.7%
Japanese	796,700	0.3%
korean	1,076,872	0.4%
Vietnamese	1,122,528	0.4%
Other Asians	1,285,234	0.5%
Native Hawaiian Pacific Islander	398,835	0.1%
Native Hawaiian	140,652	%
Samoan	91,029	%
Some Other Race	15,359,073	5.5%
Guamanian or Chamorro	58,240	%
Two or More Races (Bi-racial)	6,826,228	2.4%
Other Pacific Islanders	108,914	%

THEODUS JORDAN

Short Version Of Resume

Theodus J. Jordan

P.O. Box 840 • Boston, Massachusetts 02130   Tel: (617) 524-9598
                                                      (617) 230-3612

Objective: A position with a public or private agency
               in need of an effective administrator,
               program coordinator, counselor, and
               teacher.

Education: University of Alabama, Birmingham,
               AL Bachelor of Science in Sociology-
               Anthropology/ Psychology   1971

               Stamford University/Boston University,
               Bridgewater State, Boston, MA
               Master of Arts in Theology/Philosophy/
               Education Administration/   1975
               Mass Communications   1991

               Columbia   Southern   University,
               Orange Beach, AL Candidate for PhD
               (Philosophy)   Present

Experience: Boston and Cambridge Public Schools,
               Boston and Cambridge, MA   1980 to Present

Educator

               In addition to instruction, provide student counseling,
               classroom management, discipline, and administrative
               assistance to Principals.

               Eliot Congregational Church   Boston, MA
               Administrator/Associate Minister   1976 to Present

Develop effective programs; perform outreach development planning; implement workshops; lecture and instruct in professional training programs.

Prepare and administer budget, supervise building restorations, and developed and implemented educational and employment programs as well as community health and antipoverty programs.

University of Alabama   Birmingham, AL
Research assistant

Collected, analyzed, and interpreted statistical data for study entitled, "The Effects of Fluoridation in the City's Water Supply on the Community," for the Department of Community Dentistry. (Comprehensive background in investigative/research experience)

University of Alabama Birmingham,   AL
Personnel coordinator/health counselor   1972 to 1976

Coordinated interoffice and field activities; investigated health and social condition problems of welfare participants in a $6-million, federally-funded heart study program involving 110,000 people.

Military: United States Marine Corps Reserve   (1977-1983).
               HONORABLE DISCHARGED   1979

Other:

- ◆ C urr ently cer tified—Commonw ealth of Massachusetts—principal/teacher (Social Studies and Behavioral Sciences, History, English)—Grades 9-12, 6-12, respectively
- ◆ Holds GSA Rating of GS-0360-12 & GSA-0360-11 (Equal Opportunity Specialist)

THEODUS JORDAN

- Supervisor of GSA Federal Agency—Supervised a crew of six individuals

- While completing Master's program and continued graduate study at Harvard University and Boston University, held a variety of positions, including Organizer/Field Manager Fair Share, Inc., Boston, MA
- Field supervisor—Boston Herald American Newspaper
- Sales manager—Central Systems (copy equipment)

Computer Skills: Attended a twelve-week course in introduction to computer operations and office specialist operations. Course included introduction to PCs, Microsoft Office 97 (MS Word, MS Excel, MS Access, MS PowerPoint, MS Outlook), keyboarding, and Job Search Workshop. Veterans Technical Training Institute (Vet Tech), Boston, MA—1999.

Affiliations: National Association for the Advancement of Colored Peoples

Alpha Phi Omega National Fraternity; National Urban League;

Phi Lambda Sigma Honor Society; United Ministerial Association

{Long Version of Resume}

THEODUS J. JORDAN P.O. Box 840
Jamaica Plain, Massachusetts 02130
Phone (508) 588-6443

OBJECTIVE

A position in human services and support activities with a public or private agency in need of an effective administrator, program coordinator and counselor for areas of human resource development, management, or personnel assistance programs. Also teacher or instructor.

QUALIFICATIONS

...   Seventeen years of experience as an administrator, coordinator, organizer, and educator within health, educational, religious, social and community programs.

...   Bachelor of Science in Sociology/Anthropology/Psychology.

...   Master of Arts in Theology/Education.

...   Certificate in Education Administration.

...   Certified Teacher

...   Expertise in:

- Counseling
- Team building, group dynamics and sensing techniques.
- Advertising and promotional programs for fund raising, recruiting, and Special needs campaigns.
- Motivation and development of individuals or groups especially
- Disadvantaged.

...   Organization of research study programs involving large volunteer group participation.

Published
Author of a book entitled *The Contributions of Black Theology to Contemporary Thought*, Vantage Press, and N.Y. 1987.

...   A task-oriented, self-starting professional with strong public speaking and writing skills.

Educator
Boston Public Schools/Cambridge Public School (1979-1992).

. . .   Plan, prepare, and develop classroom instruction material for courses in History, Science, Math, English, Social Studies, and Reading for high school and middle school students.
. . .   In addition to instruction, provide student counseling, classroom management, discipline, and administrative assistant to the principal.

Administrators/Associate Minister
Eliot Congregational Church, Boston, Massachusetts; also a pastor, Southern
Baptist Church (1979-1991).

General Information:
Originally started career as assistant minister in Alabama, and after completing seven years as pastor, assistant pastor and administrator of congregation in Alabama, relocated to the Boston area.

Responsibilities and accomplishments include:
. . .   Developed effective programs to provide a resource, educational, recreational, and counseling center for the community's day-to-day life.
. . .   Performed outreach and development planning; implemented workshops, and lectured and instructed in professional development training program.
. . .   Implemented adults' and young people's educational activities for a 3,500-member congregation in an urban setting.
. . .   Administered and taught ongoing senior citizens program.
. . .   Counseled youth and young adults and planned and coordinates community projects with view to upgrading living conditions and improving community/church relations.
. . .   Prepared and administered budget, supervised building restorations and developed and implemented educational and employment programs.
. . .   Developed a community health program and sponsored an antipoverty program designed to improve the economy of the community.

Personnel coordinator/Health counselor
University of Alabama, Birmingham, Alabama (1971-1976)

...   Was assigned to an integrated federally funded $60-million project
        which involved the design and organization of a heart study program
        involving approximately 110,000 people.
...   Interviewed prospective participants and gathered case histories to
        evaluate the eligibility and dedication of applicants to comply with
        the program for its duration.
...   Coordinated interoffice and field activities and investigated health
        and social condition problems of welfare participants.

Research Assistant
University of Alabama, Birmingham, Alabama

...   The collection, analysis, and interpretation of statistical data for
        a study entitled, "The Effects of Fluoridation in the City's Water
        Supply on the Community," for the Department of Community
        Dentistry.

Program Counselor
New England College of Optometry (March 1993-Present)

...   Duties include responsibilities for implementing Counseling,
        recruitment and outreach activities related to the Optometric Career
        Access Program (OCAP) grant, under the direction of the Director
        of Minority Student Services.

OTHER AREAS OF EXPERIENCE

While completing Master's program and continued graduate study at
Harvard and Boston Universities, held a variety of positions including:

Organizer/Field Manager—Fair Share, Inc., Boston, Massachusetts

...   Contacted business, religious, and community leaders as well
        educators and homeowners while coordinating and promoting this
        fund raising project in Roxbury, Mattapan, and Dorchester areas.

THEODUS JORDAN

EDUCATION

University of Alabama, Birmingham, Alabama

Bachelor of Science in Sociology/Anthropology/Psychology, June 1971

Graduate and Post-Graduate Studies:

Samford University, Birmingham, Alabama
Master of Arts in Theology/Philosophy/Education, June 1975

Cambridge College, Cambridge, Massachusetts, 2007
Masters/Education/Counseling Psychology

Doctor of Ministry: Gordon Cromwell Theological Seminary (Accepted)

Estonian Baptist Seminary, Alabama
Homiletics, Old and New Testaments

Harvard University, Massachusetts
Etymology/Word Origin (1977)

Boston University, Massachusetts
Ethics, Education, Old Testament (1979)

Additional Education:

Bridgewater State College, Massachusetts, State of Massachusetts
—Education Administration

Eastern Nazarene College Continuing Education (1989-1991). Teacher Certificate (5) State of Massachusetts

Additional courses:

Dale Carnegie
Effective Speech, Leadership and Management Course (1977-1978)

Dumaine Speed Reading Course (1978-1979) ACTIVITIES
Tennis, table games, football, basketball, martial arts, running, reading, music, dancing, and writing children's stories.

REFERENCES
Available

BIO.

Theodus J Jordan

The author was born in a northeastern city about sixty-five miles outside of Birmingham, Alabama, called Gadsden (Etowah County) on June 12, 19_. However, he grew up in St. Clair County, in a place called Ragland, Alabama. Ragland sets about forty-miles south of Gadsden. He moved there when he was 2 or 3 years old. His father was a laborer in a cement factory called the National Cement Company. There were seven siblings. He falls as the last one. Two are deceased, as so are both his parents.

This author was educated in St. Clair County, Newtown Junior High School—a segregated school where he was bused throughout his entire school experience in order to achieve *segregation*. Eventually, he graduated from the St. Clair County Training High School in Pell City, Alabama. This high school was about 20 miles from his home even as there was a "white high school" in his own town, less than five miles away from his home. He was called to the ministry the last year of High School and went straight to the Estonian Baptist Seminary in Birmingham, Alabama. (A school for educating black preachers, at any age, during that time).

After receiving a Bachelor's Certificate, he felt the need to enter a four year liberal arts school call Daniel Payne College, also of Birmingham, Alabama. After two years, he was awarded an Associate's degree. It was then he entered into the University of Alabama in Birmingham. Here, he graduated with a full accredited bachelor's (B.S.) degree in Sociology-Anthropology and minored in Psychology and Philosophy . . . . During that time, one could have double majors and minors. From here he entered graduate school at a well known "white suburban" Southern Baptist School called Stamford University in Mountain Brook, Alabama. Religion/Philosophy/Education/Languages were his areas of concentration. The author's graduate (MA) degree was granted in 1979.

He worked for University of Alabama in Birmingham as a Health-Counselor for almost eight years and **pastored** or was the **assistant pastor** of four distinct Baptist churches prior to relocating to Boston, Massachusetts, in the latter part of seventies, or early eighties, to further his graduate studies. He enrolled in the Harvard Continuation Education program where he began to study *linguistics and etymology*. He eventually took substitute-teaching jobs for the Cambridge Public Schools system because now he was in need of money. Then he went on to the Boston Public Schools system where he eventually became a regular classroom teacher for while. Then, he moved to the Brockton Public Schools system . . . . Later, returning to the Boston Public schools. Meanwhile, Jordan—this author, continued in his preaching just as he had done in the South.

He became the pastor of the Southern Baptist Church of Roxbury. Prior to this, since coming to Boston, Jordan was the assistant pastor of the Eliot Congregational Church of Roxbury, under the notorious Reverend Anthony Campbell. At present, he is an <u>associated</u> pastor with the Messiah Baptist Church in Brockton, Massachusetts.

Since coming to Boston, Jordan, the author has acquired 4 teachers' certificates from the State of Massachusetts, two administrative certificates as a Principal and Assistant Principal and/or Headmaster. He has attended the Northeastern School for Diagnostic Reading . . . obtained the Certificate of Graduate Studies from Bridgewater State College (University). Jordan has acquired another Master of Arts degree from Cambridge College, in Education/ Counseling Psychology (2007). This author has completed all but a final project from the Graduate School of Communication at Boston University in Broadcast Journalism, but, no degree was ever conferred . . . . Jordan has been accepted as a Doctoral (D.Min.) student at the Gordon-Crowell Theological Seminary in Hamilton, Massachusetts—though non-matriculating at present). Jordan, in 2008, was also accepted into the PH.D Educational Psychology program at Cappella University, Minneapolis, Minnesota. However, at present, he is not matriculating.

Finally, Jordan has written and published one other text prior to **this work**, in 1987, entitled *"The Contributions of Black Theology to Contemporary Thought"*. He plans to republish this book in the near future.

He is,

Theodus J. Jordan,
<u>**Servant of God!**</u>

INDEX